How to Be a *Better* Procrastinator!

Dr. Patrick Sanaghan

Tomorrow is the busiest day of the week.
—Spanish Proverb

CHAPTERS

Introduction

Procrastination is, hands down, our favorite form of self-sabotage.

—Alyce P. Cornyn Selby

I am a procrastinator and have been all my adult life. But I am a very *productive* procrastinator.

Although I struggle with the procrastination habit, I have graduated from college, earned a doctorate, written or co-authored twelve books, and written over fifty published papers, articles, and monographs. Before the COVID-19 pandemic, I had a thriving consulting practice that put me on the road about 150 days a year. Now I spend about 30 hours a week on Zoom or Skype meetings. I am busy, pretty accomplished—and I still procrastinate.

I have missed writing deadlines, filed my income taxes late several times, and often dither over details such as making flight arrangements and writing invoices. I put off these things until the very last minute. Like many other procrastinators, I suffer or live with stress, anxiety, guilt, and feelings of being overwhelmed by my procrastination tendencies. But things have gotten much better as I have learned to manage this terrible habit over many years.

I understand procrastination in a deep way and have written this book for others who have the procrastination habit and want to learn how to manage it. I strongly believe that this mean habit never goes away—ever. The best we can do is neutralize its impact with lots of practices, protocols, mindfulness, and discipline.

Procrastination is a very tough habit to deal with. Never forget this. It is a pernicious habit that is always present. You need to pay attention and manage it every day to keep the procrastination gremlin at bay.

It's a lot like monitoring your ideal weight. You have to exercise regularly, *especially* when you don't feel like exercising. You have to carefully watch what you eat and avoid your seductions (e.g., ice cream, chocolate cake, beer, pizza). You have to pay attention and be disciplined or the pounds will magically reappear.

Using some of the ideas in this book can help you manage this negative habit, but there are no shortcuts or silver bullets. It will be hard work but almost always well worth the effort. When you begin to experience the accomplishment of the things that matter most to you, it can create a positive sense of accomplishment and a powerful sense of momentum toward achieving your goals.

Procrastination has damaged millions of careers. It can impact people's health—think of the consequences of delay in going to the doctor or dentist. It has cost people billions of dollars in late income tax fees, credit card payment penalties, missed scholarship and grant deadlines, and more (Combs, 2011).

Almost everyone procrastinates about something, but chronic procrastinators, who constitute around 20 % of the population, procrastinate about almost everything. It becomes a lifestyle for millions of people and permeates their personal and professional lives (Steel, 2007; Ferrari, 2010; Combs, 2011).

> The dread of doing the task uses up more time and energy
> than doing the task itself.
>
> —Rita Emmett

Fixing Dictionaries

I want to share several definitions of procrastination so that we begin to understand its complexity and get on the same page about what we are dealing with.

The word "procrastination" comes from the Latin words *pro*—which means forward, forth or in favor of—and *crastinus*—which means tomorrow. Procrastination is putting something off until later, usually something you don't want to do.

Merriam-Webster defines procrastination as "to put off *intentionally* the doing of something that *should* be done.

Dr. Piers Steel, who is an academic, a psychoanalyst, and a big name in the field of procrastination studies, describes procrastination as "*to voluntarily delay an intended course of action despite expecting to be worse off for the delay*."

Another big-name researcher is Dr. Timothy Pychyl from Carleton University in Canada. He describes procrastination as a *"self inflicted wound that gradually chips away at our most valuable resource, time."*

Lastly, Neil Fiore (2007), author of *The Now Habit* and my favorite author on procrastination, defines procrastination as "a mechanism for coping with the anxiety associated with starting or completing any task or decision."

I think these definitions share some common elements.

Procrastinators delay or put off things until later. Usually they delay things they find unpleasant, overwhelming, or anxiety-producing. But here's the thing: they do it knowing they will probably be worse off for the delay. That's what makes procrastination so mean. Avoidance hurts procrastinators down the road, and they know it—but they do it anyway.

What doesn't get mentioned very often in the literature is the fact that procrastination is hugely rewarding. You experience almost instant relief from the noxious or difficult emotions you are feeling about the task you are facing. This is an important point. If this sense of a relief reward weren't present, many of us wouldn't procrastinate. Why would we need to? Bad habits like procrastination have an immediate reward, and that is what makes them so powerful.

The reward relief experience creates a vicious cycle and powerful habit that is hard to break or manage. Steel describes it as a voluntary act, but it sure doesn't feel that way to me. Often the avoidance behavior happens so quickly that it doesn't seem to be a conscious act, let alone a voluntary one.

Sometimes small tasks can feel like the most difficult thing to do. For example, as a consultant, I have many clients, and I find invoicing my clients a daunting task because of the little details involved. Each client has different forms to fill out, protocols to follow, and practices that need to be adhered to. I often put off my billing process for a long time. All these details are daunting for me. That may sound silly, but it's true.

If I have a complicated invoicing process—say a two-week-long trip during which I work with several clients, and each has different charges that need to be calculated (e.g., how much each client pays for flights, different consulting rates for for-profit clients versus nonprofit clients, and how many parking-lot days to charge each client)—I can really procrastinate, even though by completing the invoicing process, *I get paid.*

It might sound strange to a nonprocrastinator. "How can you delay getting paid?" But it's an accurate snapshot of the procrastination dynamic. This is how it usually works: a procrastinator has a task (usually an unpleasant one) to do. They begin to feel anxious, stressed, and overwhelmed. Some even describe it as dread.

To avoid these negative emotions, they run away and do something that feels better. This temporarily relieves the bad feelings. The natural tendency when dealing with these negative emotions is to avoid them quickly.

Unpleasant Task↘

(Repeat Cycle)↗

Negative Feelings
and Thoughts↘

**↑Instant Relief
from Negative
Feelings**

Avoidance of the
Thoughts and Feelings↙

↖Avoid the Unpleasant Task

I get overwhelmed by all the details and usually delay doing the invoicing, even though I have invoiced clients for thirty years. I know it, and I still do it! But I've gotten much better over time, utilizing some of the practices I will share in this book.

I still don't like invoicing, and this is an important notion. I have learned to manage my negative emotions and *do it anyway*. This is a theme we will discuss a lot in the book, because one of the most powerful strategies for dealing with procrastination is to experience the feelings you are having and not allow your feelings to dictate your behavior over and over again.

The only way out is through.
—Robert Frost

Procrastinators also engage in silly self-talk. See if these excuses sound familiar:

- I don't have enough time to do it well today, so I will wait until tomorrow, when I will have enough time. (*Who are you kidding?*)

- I know that I will feel like doing it tomorrow. (*One of the great lies of all time.*)

- I almost always work better under pressure. (*Another whopper of a lie, and a pervasive one.*)

- I can never get all this done, so why start now? (*We give in to the feeling of being overwhelmed.*)

- I'm just too tired now; I will do it later when I have more energy. (*Another example of who are you kidding?*)

- It's too late to start. I will wait until I have some real time to do this. (*One of my favorite excuses.*)

You get the idea. We have scores of these silly lines bouncing around in our heads. They enable us to engage in procrastination. We need to pay attention to this inner dialogue because these excuses are the telltale signs of the procrastination habit kicking into high gear.

Although I will share a fair amount of research about procrastination, this is not an academic tome in tone or tenor. It's a book written by a procrastinator for procrastinators. It will provide strategies, protocols, and practices that have worked for me and many fellow procrastinators. They are battle tested. If you select the right ones for you and apply them diligently, they will almost always work.

A Caution

Too often, procrastinators are way too hard on themselves. They constantly berate themselves, are self-critical, feel guilty, and experience too many regrets for one lifetime.

Try mightily to be more self-compassionate and let go of the mean self-criticism, because it simply is not helpful. The notion of self-compassion is an important one for procrastinators, and I will describe it in some detail later. Research indicates that it is one of the most effective strategies for dealing with procrastination (Pychyl, 2013).

This book is not intended to make you feel even worse about your procrastination habit. My intention is to help you understand how pernicious and mean procrastination is and to suggest ways to manage this habit so that you can feel better about yourself, accomplish more of the things that matter to you, and even be a happier person.

Delaying gratification is a process of scheduling the pain and pleasure of life in such a way as to enhance the pleasure by meeting and experiencing the pain first and getting it over with.
It's the only decent way to live.
—M. Scott Peck

Peck's words are powerful and capture the essence of the difficult journey forward. We have to be committed to live with the pain caused by our very uncomfortable feelings and emotions, and not have them dictate our avoidance behavior.

I am not a psychologist, so these suggestions don't have a therapeutic or psychodynamic perspective. For deeply chronic procrastinators, I strongly suggest getting support from a therapist. Unfortunately, a lot of people simply can't afford the money or time investment to seek extensive therapy for the reasons why they procrastinate so often.

I will name some great psychologists throughout the book, who deeply understand procrastination and whose ideas can be very helpful. They have informed my thinking and helped me with my own procrastination habit. I am not "cured" of it; I manage it every day and wrestle with it often. So I want to manage expectations here: this book is not a cure-all or a miracle solution.

I also realize that some people suffer with ADHD, a neurodevelopmental disorder characterized by impulsivity and inattention, which can be debilitating. Other readers might be clinically depressed. Both groups would benefit from psychotherapy, counseling, and even medication. I am not saying that the ideas presented in this book cannot help these individuals, but they face unique challenges if they are also procrastinators.

This book is for most of us who procrastinate a lot—but not always—on difficult, uncomfortable, new, and challenging things. I have managed my procrastination over many years of trial and error. I am familiar with all the ideas in this book and have tried many of them. I have also coached many successful senior executives and leaders through their procrastination tendencies, and I have learned a lot from their struggles.

I hope you find these ideas helpful in your personal journey through procrastination land. It's not a happy place. I want to help you travel the territory, accomplish your dreams, and enjoy your life more. Good luck!

Procrastination Note

When you get down on yourself about your procrastination habit, remember that you are in good company. Leonardo da Vinci was a prolific procrastinator; he took 16 years to paint the *Mona Lisa*. So was Herman Melville, who reportedly had his wife chain him to his desk while he was struggling to write *Moby Dick*. Victor Hugo, the great French poet and novelist, had his servant strip him naked so he wouldn't go outside and procrastinate. Frank Lloyd Wright, the famous architect, drew the plans for Fallingwater, one of his greatest achievements, just two hours before meeting with his client, who was exasperated with how long it was taking Wright to provide the plans for his house. Finally, J. R. R. Tolkien suffered from perfectionism and procrastination in equal doses, spending the better part of 16 years working intermittently on *The Lord of the Rings* after the initial success of *The Hobbit* in 1937.

I am not encouraging your procrastination. I want to show you that even if we procrastinate, we still can be productive and successful. We will probably not be as prolific as these legends, but don't get down on yourself about this habit. It simply is not helpful.

How This Book Is Organized

Chapter 1

In this brief chapter, I share significant concepts about procrastination. It's important to understand the powerful and often hidden dynamics of procrastination, so we know what we are dealing with. Tens of millions of people suffer from this mean habit. Understanding the underlying dynamics is an essential first step in the learning journey.

Procrastination is the Art of Keeping up with Yesterday
—Don Marquis

Chapter 2

In this chapter I discuss the four levers of procrastination: (a) the power of habits; (b) the notion of willpower, its myths, and its realities; (c) how to develop attention and focus; and (d) the importance of mindfulness and self-compassion when dealing with our habit.

Chapter 3

In this chapter I share 21 powerful practices, strategies, and tools that are worth considering in the battle against procrastination. With this mean habit, you need all the ideas you can get. The intention of this chapter is to build a powerful and diverse toolbox of ideas to use.

A caution: Many procrastinators have a strong tendency to try too many things and fail at most of them. Don't fall into this trap. I strongly suggest that you read the ideas and pick *one* that resonates with you—whether intellectually, imaginatively, or emotionally. Try it for week and see what happens. If it works, then keep at it for a month. By then it should come a little more naturally. I will talk later about the power of habits and how long they can take to create. They don't just happen overnight; they take a lot of time and patience.

This will require some effort and discipline, but it is worth the time invested. Over a year, if you can utilize several of these practices, I hope you will be in a different and better place with your procrastination habit.

Chapter 4

This chapter has 38 procrastination hacks or shortcuts to use when you start to procrastinate, or to prevent you from procrastinating. Little things can have a surprisingly big impact, so think about using some of them and building up your toolbox. Most are easier to operationalize than the 21 practices in chapter 3, so you might want to start with some of these hacks.

Chapter 5

I have created a procrastination quiz informed by the research on procrastination and my own experience. It's informal but will act like an MRI, helping you gain deep insight about how you tend to procrastinate. People who have taken it have reported that it has helped them better understand their particular procrastination habit. With this understanding, they have selected strategies and hacks to combat the ways they procrastinate.

Chapter 6

This chapter is composed of mini chapters that are quick reads full of practical advice. It's designed for procrastinators who want to read something they can apply right away. The mini chapters are:

- How to Say No to Others' Requests

- Ten Big Procrastination Strategies

- The Procrastination Strategy Matrix

- Small Wisdoms

Appendices

In this section, I share my work schedule, which helps me be a very productive procrastinator. I am not setting myself up as some kind of exemplar of productivity, but my clients have found it helpful to see the specific structures and protocols I have built that enhance my effectiveness and neutralize my procrastination tendencies. I hope you find it useful also.

I also share my favorite five strategies for combatting procrastination. I provide a toolbox with information on many apps that can help manage distractions. And, in a short section, I share some information about the Stoics, who have much wisdom to share about procrastination, discipline, and managing emotions.

How to Use This Book

I suggest that you start anywhere you want. This book doesn't need to be read cover to cover. You might want to check out the small wisdoms in the mini chapters first. They're quick reads, and you will get a sense of the practicality of the ideas in the rest of the book. Or you might go right to the procrastination quiz because it's interesting and easy to take. Or you might review the hacks chapter quickly.

You get the idea—do what feels right to you. The point is to get started somewhere—anywhere—and read ASAP. This book was written specifically for procrastinators, and it is organized in small chunks so that it is a quick, digestible read. I believe that if you give it 10 minutes, you will find practical and useful advice.

You will see a lot of quotations sprinkled throughout the book. I really like quotations, because they are usually short and powerful, and because they capture the essence of important themes that need consideration. They can also be motivating for some people. Use what works for you. I have several quotations posted in my office to encourage me to move forward.

How did it get so late so soon?

—Dr. Seuss

Chapter 1
Important Concepts to Understand

If you are going to manage your procrastination habit, you need to be a student of the game. Learn as much as you can about the often hidden and underlying dynamics that help create procrastination habits. The following concepts and frameworks will help you learn about the complexity of procrastination without getting lost in the details of it.

Parkinson's Law

In the 1950s, Cyril Northcote Parkinson, an economist, published an article describing Parkinson's law: Work expands to fill the time available for its completion. For example, if you give yourself a week to complete a task, it will often take the entire week to complete, even though it could probably be done in a day or two.

Think about that for a minute. A project will expand to fit any time frame you have allotted for its completion. We often make things much more complicated than they are. We tell ourselves we will have plenty of time, and then delay getting started because we have "all the time in the world."

There is a lot of research about college students and procrastination. In some studies, students were given assignments at the beginning of the semester, with deadlines that were far away (Ferrari, 2010; Steel, 2007; Pychyl, 2013). Most waited until the last two days of the semester to complete their assignments, and they experienced a great deal of stress and anxiety as the deadlines drew near.

This describes the procrastinator's dilemma many of us face. We often wait till the very end and then race to the finish line, exhausted, stressed, and not sure about the quality of the work we produced. We need to get really good at creating intermediate deadlines that come sooner rather than later, encouraging us not to wait until the very end to get started.

A deadline is like a fire. When it's far away, it's pretty and warm. As we move closer to the fire, it gets warmer and warmer, until we are right on top of the fire and it's really hot. Procrastinators need to move up their deadlines so we feel a little heat from the very beginning. Once again, having intermediate "mini" deadlines is often an effective strategy for procrastinators.

Suggestions on How to Manage Parkinson's Law

Before you create a realistic deadline for a task, consider discussing the following three questions with a thought partner.

- *How long has an assignment like this taken me in the past?* This should give you an informed picture of what is realistic. Then think about setting a deadline as soon as you can. If you set it too far off, you will probably wait until the deadline is looming.

- *Can I do this assignment in a different way?* For example, instead of going through several written drafts for a paper, all of which take real time, you could dictate a rough draft on a digital voice recorder and have it transcribed. That way, you begin with a pretty good draft you can further refine. I use this technique a lot because I can talk very fast, but I can't write fast. Another example is clearing and organizing your garage, a task most of us love to procrastinate on. Ask a friend to help you, and return the favor. Bottom line: try to be creative about *how* to accomplish the task. That's why thought partners are so helpful, because they can add a different perspective we simply don't see or think about.

- *What obstacles can I anticipate?* Take ten minutes to think through some of the potential barriers that could get in the way of completing the task. Then strategize how to avoid or neutralize those challenges before you start. I will talk about this strategy in some detail later in the book.

The Planning Fallacy

The planning fallacy is the kissing cousin of Parkinson's law. It was proposed by I. Daniel Kahneman, winner of the Nobel Memorial Prize in Economic Sciences. He found in his research that we tend to underestimate the time and resources we need to achieve our goals. We do this because most of us have an optimistic bias, and plan only for best-case scenarios. We often assume that everything will go perfectly, which rarely happens.

This is dangerous for procrastinators because we will often get stuck, frustrated, and overwhelmed when our original estimates are way off base. This kicks in the procrastination habit big-time, and we tend to avoid the task or quit it entirely. Sound familiar?

> Mistakes weigh heavily on those who expect nothing
> but good fortune.
> —Seneca

It is also helpful to always remember Hofstadter's law, which states, "It will always take longer than we expect." When a task does take longer, we usually assume that external forces—multiple interruptions, the failures of others—caused the delay and not any issues on our part.

We systematically overestimate how much we can actually accomplish—by a lot. We predict that a task will take less time and energy than it does. We predict that we will get better outcomes than we actually do.

Let me provide a couple of whoppers.

- The newest span of the Bay Bridge connecting San Francisco with Oakland was budgeted for $1.4 billion. It ended costing $6.4 billion and was completed six years later than predicted.

- The Sydney Opera House in Australia, one of the most notable buildings in the world, was budgeted for $7 million. It took $102 million and was completed 10 years later than predicted.

- The England–France Chunnel and the Denver Airport both went over budget by billions and took much longer than ever imagined.

So procrastinators are not alone in dealing with the planning fallacy. We need to compensate for this powerful tendency because it's always present in our personal and professional lives.

here are five major strategies you can use to help with the planning fallacy. Some of these strategies are similar to the suggestions I shared for managing Parkinson's law.

- Look at your past efforts to predict how long a task will take. For example, if it took you 15 hours to research and write a 10-page paper the last time you produced one, there is a very good chance your next 10-page paper will take roughly the same amount of time.

- Get some help. If you have little experience with writing 10-page papers—or fixing plumbing or painting a house—then ask someone who has done it. You can also watch a video about it.

- Think about how long another person might take to do a similar task. This moves you from a subjective view of your capacity to a more objective, realistic view of another person's capacity. Surprisingly, we tend to estimate for others more effectively than for ourselves.

- Think about all the worst-case scenarios that could occur in completing the task. Hofstadter suggests that we double our estimate about how much time the task will take. That resonates deeply with me, in my extensive strategic-planning experience.

- Get a third party's perspective about the task. An outsider will have less subjective bias about the project, since they are not psychologically involved. Obviously, they need to be familiar with the work involved so their estimate is not pulled out of thin air. Soliciting another person's perspective doesn't take much time, but it can save you a lot of time and stress in the end.

Hyperbolic Discounting

Richard Herrnstein, a psychologist at Harvard, first introduced the concept of hyperbolic discounting. This is the tendency for most people, especially procrastinators, to choose smaller and sooner rewards over larger, later rewards.

There has been a great deal of research conducted over the years to investigate this cognitive bias. Most of research found that we tend to overvalue immediate rewards, sometimes dramatically so. For example, if given the choice of getting $100 today or $120 in a month, most people choose the $100 now. But when the same choice is given with a one-year instead of a one-month interval, they usually choose the $120 in the future.

When we procrastinate, we opt for the instant gratification of enjoying ourselves or alleviating a bad feeling now, rather than the future reward of accomplishing what we set out to do.

There is dramatic research (Backman 2020) showing that when people get the opportunity to save money right away with a 401(k) plan—even with matching company funds, which are really "free "money—many people will not invest. One study indicated as many as 44% of all people with the opportunity to invest in a 401(k) plan do not do so, because retirement seems too far off to be worth investing in now.

Many people discount the value of their future health and make choices that satisfy their immediate desires, such as eating a rich dessert or smoking, that will have negative long-term effects.

First, we need a realistic perspective about how long or difficult a task will be. Second, we need to think about what could go wrong so we don't set ourselves up for failure. We *love* short-term rewards and instant gratification. Unfortunately, this gets in the way of accomplishing important long-term goals.

A Couple of Interesting Concepts to Think About

The following ideas have informed me about the complexities of my procrastination habit and provided me with deep insight into the pervasiveness of procrastination and what is realistic to accomplish.

Steven Pressfield—The War of Art *(2012)*

Pressfield believes that everyone struggles with self-sabotage (e.g., thoughts such as *I am not smart enough to write a book, I am going to be a failure with this project because I don't really know what I am doing*). He calls these self-defeating thoughts *resistance.*

Resistance has many forms—such as procrastination, self-medication, fear, and victimhood—and it's always present, in his view This is a powerful and daunting theme in many of his books. Resistance never goes away, just like the procrastination urge itself, and he believes we will be fighting it all our lives. All the people who are trying to be creative, to do something different from what they are used to, or otherwise are taking a risk meet resistance daily and answer it with the self-doubt and criticism that we create in our heads. Sound familiar? The internal voices and self-talk are ever present, and we need to learn to ignore them.

The most effective way to tone down the voices is to act. Pressfield advises that the most powerful strategy is to do the work and quit dithering. He asks us to consider two important questions:

- *How badly do I want this?* You need to be totally committed to what you want to accomplish. Having a meaningful purpose can create the motivation to endure the frustration, aggravation, and even pain of working toward your goals

- *Why do you want this?* Is it for external reward and recognition, or is this something that is a passion for you? Are you willing to pay the price to accomplish it?

In short, your dream, aspiration, and even ambition must matter in deep and mighty ways. Pressfield believes that the biggest barrier to our success is fear of success.

If we are going to achieve our dreams and openly face our constant internal resistance, we need to become professionals. His idea about professionals isn't about roles (e.g., dentist, lawyer, or teacher). It's about a powerful mindset. We need to be pros and do the work whether we feel like it or not. We need to work through big fears about what we can accomplish.

Pros don't wait for motivation—they act. This is a big theme in productivity and procrastination research. Pros get started even when they are fearful. They apply consistent activities to their aspirations— writing 10 pages a day, calling that first client, asking others for help— and are persistent in their efforts. They do the work that needs to be done every day.

I think Pressfield's ideas are intriguing, even counterintuitive, yet they resonate with me as a procrastinator. The idea that resistance will always be present is a disheartening one, but it feels real.

I think about my own self-doubt as an author every time I begin a book. I thought I would be more comfortable after completing twelve books, but I'm not. Nevertheless, I continue to write and will do so until I can't.

Pressfield provides an interesting story about the late, great actor Henry Fonda, who threw up every time before he went on stage. But he got on stage anyway and shared his craft. The great Boston Celtics basketball center, Bill Russell, did the same thing before every game.

> The warrior and the artist live by the same code of necessity, which dictates that the battle must be fought anew every day.
> —Steven Pressfield

Lastly and hopefully, Pressfield asserts that "unforeseen forces" will enlist in our cause. Powerful forces come to our aid as we dedicate ourselves to our craft. He believes there is "magic" in starting a project. We can expect a lot of positive things to occur as we become pros and capture our dreams. This is a tad mystical for me personally, but worth believing for some people.

Whatever you can do, or dream you can, begin it. Boldness has
genius, power and magic in it. Begin it now.

—Goethe

The bottom line for Pressfield is that resistance is ever present. Acknowledge this, even if it's disappointing, because it's normal. Do the work any way you can. Action is the strategic wedge that enables us to break free of resistance and get meaningful things done.

The Whirlwind

This outstanding idea comes from the book *The 4 Disciplines of Execution* (2014). It has enabled me to help normalize the feelings of stress, frustration, and being overwhelmed I often experience, as do many of my clients as they try to focus on their work and get something done.

Basically, the notion of the whirlwind is that it takes a great deal of effort, time, energy, and hard work to keep any organization functioning. Many meetings take place, communication processes are required to inform stakeholders, projects need to be managed, problems emerge out of nowhere and must be solved—all these activities and more keep the organization afloat.

The authors believe it takes about 80% of a leader's attention, effort, and time just to keep the organization functioning on a daily basis. Think about this.

If 80% of all the energy, attention, and time is already spent, that leaves the leader with 20% of their time to do other, hopefully strategic stuff. Twenty percent is not a whole lot to get other things done. Therefore, an organization needs to be very disciplined and focus on the handful of crucial actions it needs to accomplish to move the organization forward.

I believe this has a direct connection to our personal and professional lives. If 80% of our time is already "spent" (e.g., family time;

responsibilities; commitments; going to our churches, mosques, and synagogues; exercise; school; home projects), then we have only 20% of our time for the most important stuff.

Therefore, we have to be able to prioritize our top goals and be disciplined and focused on the things that truly matter. We can't do everything we want because there isn't enough time to do it. It is as simple, stark, and powerful as it sounds.

Obviously, we can be really busy with lots of stuff, feel overwhelmed because we can't make the right choices, and feel disappointed in ourselves for not accomplishing what matters.

> Its not enough to be busy,so are ants.
> The question is: What are you busy about?
> —Henry David Thoreau

One of the most important themes of this book is the critical need to figure out what really matters to us personally and professionally. This will be hard to do, but you must commit to doing what matters. Otherwise you will be busy, overwhelmed, distracted, and disappointed, and you will not get meaningful things done.

Having a clear and realistic sense of what you want to accomplish in a year, month, and week is hard to do, but it is an essential task if we are to manage the whirlwind and reach our most important goals.

> Busyness is a decision.
> —Kierkegaard

Having a Thomas Edison State of Mind

Years ago, I read a biography of Thomas Edison and was fascinated by his story and achievements. We have all been taught about his inventions. He quit school when he was 12 years old and also lost 75%

of his hearing at that time. He was given 1,093 US patents during his lifetime. His contributions to the light bulb, motion picture camera, and phonograph, among many other inventions, helped modernize the world. He established a "think/invention tank" in Menlo Park, New Jersey, where he worked with many other people, called fellow "muckers," and created a place where imagination and practicality got married.

What makes Edison so interesting, besides his many accomplishments, is his attitude toward life. He was very curious about many things and didn't care where ideas came from, because he believed others had great ideas also. He was persistent and tenacious about his work, a workaholic. He had many failures and made a lot of mistakes as he invented some extraordinary things.

Legend tells us that his great quotation about failing ten thousand times wasn't about failure at all, but part of his learning journey. He saw the ten thousand attempts as helping him eliminate the ways that didn't work. I believe that this is a counterintuitive and exceptional perspective and has relevance to our procrastination habit. If Edison had been self-critical, like many procrastinators, he would have given up around the thousandth attempt, if not much sooner. But he didn't. He persisted because he was a learner.

As procrastinators try to manage our habit over time, we will have some failures and make some mistakes. That's a guarantee. What's important to remember is to look at failure as part of a learning journey.

Learning has a price. We won't get it right the first time, so we need to manage our own expectations carefully. You will try some of the ideas and practices in this book, and some won't work for you. Don't give up. Persist a little longer and see what happens.

We didn't develop our habit overnight. It took years to get to this place, and it will take some time and effort (if not ten thousand attempts) to change our habit. Please think about how Edison saw the world. He was curious and persistent. Both qualities are helpful companions in our procrastination journey.

Edison saw failure as *information*, not something negative. He believed that the mistakes were feedback that helped him discover what actually worked. When we try the strategies and practices in this book, we will fail because not everything works perfectly or quickly. If we can have an orientation toward learning about what works, it will help us learn about our own procrastination.

Opportunity is missed by most people because its dressed up in overalls and looks like work.
—Thomas Alva Edison

Chapter 2
The Four Levers of Procrastination

Give me a lever long enough and a fulcrum on which to place it and
I can move the world.
—Archimedes

The Law of the Lever and Procrastination

I want to describe a series of psychological and behavioral levers that
will enable procrastinators to achieve some advantage or leverage over
the mean habit of procrastination. This chapter will describe four powerful levers that you can use to help manage your procrastination. They
are

- understanding the power of habits

- developing focus and attention

- recognizing the myths and realities of willpower

- appreciating the vital importance of mindfulness and
  self-compassion and the role of meditation

With a deep understanding of these four levers, procrastinators can learn to use them effectively in the ongoing battle we wage to manage our procrastination habit.

In the following pages I will outline some information about the four levers for procrastination. This will not be an in-depth discussion of each one, but more of an informal summary of what they are and why they are important to understand.

These levers act as an integrated framework for procrastinators to apply to our habit. They are not separate, distinct levers isolated from each other. As you will see, they often overlap and support each other.

For example, I will explore what habits are and how they come into being, how they sustain themselves over time, and how they powerfully influence our behavior. I will talk about positive habits like mindfulness, meditation, and self-compassion, which can help us neutralize the negative power of procrastination.

Lever 1: The Power and Complexity of Habits

There are a number of authors and researchers who have written extensively about how habits work and their powerful influence in our daily lives (Duhigg, 2014; Eyal, 2014; Clear, 2018). They also discuss how difficult it can be to change a habit or create a new one.

According to researchers, habits emerge because the brain is constantly looking for ways to save effort. Left to its own devices, the brain will try to make almost any routine activity into a habit.

An efficient brain allows us to stop thinking consciously about basic behaviors, such as walking, choosing what to eat, or driving a car, so that we can devote our mental energy to higher-order thinking.

I will briefly explain how Charles Duhigg, a Pulitzer Prize winner and author of several bestselling books, including *The Power of Habit* (2012), sees our habits forming. I will add some ideas from James

Clear, who also writes about habits and procrastination. Although their ideas are aligned for the most part, understanding their slightly different views is a helpful tutorial about the power of habits.

How Habits Work—Charles Duhigg

There is some kind of cue or trigger in the environment that makes a habitual behavior unfold automatically. A cue could be a location, a certain time, a specific emotion, a pattern of behavior, or a person.

Then there is a routine, which is the behavior itself. This could be grabbing a cookie around three o'clock every day, drinking a glass of wine after dinner, or smoking a cigarette whenever you get nervous. A routine can be physical, mental, or emotional.

The reward is why habits exist. There has to be a reward to build a habit. The reward is the payoff for engaging in the routine. This could be a dopamine hit, less anxiety, or a sugar high.

How Habits Work—James Clear

James Clear, in his book *Atomic Habits* (2018), sees almost the same habit pathway that Duhigg articulates. But he adds something that enabled me to better understand how habits are formed.

The *cue* is the factor or element that activates the brain to detect the possibility of a reward or pleasure. A cue can be a sound, event, interaction, picture, or smell—anything that triggers a desire.

The desire is known as the *craving*. The craving is the emotional relevance attached to a certain cue. When you notice the cue (this can also be unconscious), the brain anticipates the opportunity for a change in your physical or emotional state. You crave the satisfaction that the change will elicit, and this craving prompts you to act.

The response is the actual behavior habit performed to elicit the change you want. Your brain prompts you to take a certain action it believes will create the feeling of satisfaction you want.

The reward is the satisfaction gained from the action taken.

Summary: The cue triggers a craving, which motivates a response, which provides a reward, which satisfies the craving and ultimately becomes associated with the cue. The cycle continues on and on.

If we generally agree on the four parts of a habit, then this is how I see the procrastination habit being formed:

- *The cue*: We are faced with a noxious, complicated, overwhelming, or boring task that causes us stress, anxiety, confusion, or dread. In short, we are very uncomfortable.

- *The craving*: This is a little counterintuitive, because most people think that a craving is a desire for something positive. With procrastination, I believe that our craving is to quickly escape the uncomfortable feeling that is our cue. The emphasis is on *quickly*—we want to escape uncomfortable feelings as fast as possible.

On the surface, this makes absolute sense. Who wouldn't want to get rid of these negative feelings? This is what makes the procrastination habit so tenacious and devious, but we pay a steep price for our temporary escape.

What we will learn is that in the moments of cravings, we can stop taking the escape path if we employ patience, protocols, practice, and mindfulness.

Our predictable routine is to get rid of the uncomfortable task somehow and put it off, even though we know it still needs to be completed. The reward is almost instant relief from our discomfort. This feels good most of the time.

Duhigg believes that habits never really disappear because they are encoded in the structure of the brain. The problem is that the brain can't tell the difference between a good habit and a bad habit.

At one point we made conscious decisions about everything: how much to eat, how much to drink, the first thing we do when we get up in the morning. Then we stopped making these choices and the behaviors became automatic. When a habit emerges, the brain stops fully participating in decision-making. It stops working so hard or diverts its focus to other tasks.

So, unless you find new routines, a habitual pattern will unfold automatically. The habit, according to Duhigg, is always lurking, waiting for the right cues and rewards. This is much like Pressfield's notion of resistance always being present.

One can understand the power of these ingrained habits when we think about how difficult it is for an alcoholic to quit drinking. It's a lifelong battle that never goes away. The same is true of heavy smokers. Research shows that most smokers try up to seven times before they finally quit smoking (Duhigg, 2012). The craving is always there, lurking right below the surface.

Becoming conscious of how the cycle of procrastination works provides us with some insight into the challenge we face. Insight is the first step. Action is what matters, and I will share a lot of practical actions to take.

The Importance of Keystone Habits

Charles Duhigg provides us with a powerful notion when he shares the idea of *keystone habits* or *super habits*. These important habits, when actively developed, can positively influence other parts of our lives.

For example, if you start to jog for an hour each morning, you will gradually get in physical shape and maybe even lose some weight.

Once you establish your jogging habit, there is a very good chance you won't overeat at dinner or drink a six-pack of beer at night, because you might be sluggish or feel hungover the next morning, and running would be difficult.

In this way, the important healthy habit of jogging can have a ripple effect in other parts of your life. You would probably also feel a sense of real accomplishment and improved self-confidence, which are added benefits. By adopting *one* healthy keystone habit, you can enhance and improve other areas of your life.

Conversely, a negative habit, like drinking too much, overeating, not exercising, or smoking could impact your physical and mental health, and maybe even your personal relationships.

Meditation is a keystone habit that can help create a sense of calm, reduce stress, improve focus, and increase awareness. I will talk more about the positive power of meditation later in the mindfulness section.

Having family dinners on a regular basis can be another keystone habit that improves family conversation and cohesion. Some research indicates that families that have dinner together regularly tend to have children with more confidence, higher grades in school, and greater emotional control (Duhigg, 2012). In addition, family dinners can open up the channels of communication and create the opportunity to discuss family values and other important things.

Keystone habits *don't* create cause-and-effect relationships, but they can cause a chain reaction of sorts that helps other good habits take hold. One example is food tracking. It can become a keystone habit when you write down what you actually eat every day. This takes some real discipline, and a support group can help with this habit. Sharing with others what you ate that day or week can make you more aware of how much you eat, when you eat, and what you eat.

The National Institutes of Health found that participants in a research study who journaled their eating habits lost twice as much weight as those who didn't. With journaling, a person can begin to notice certain routines in their eating habits, such as eating a candy bar in the late afternoon to get a jolt of energy, or binge eating in front of the TV late at night to wind down from the stress of the day.

A couple of years ago, I met with my doctor about losing some weight. One of the things he suggested was to write a food journal for a week. I didn't like the idea much, but I agreed, since I wasn't losing any weight by "trying" to.

I do a lot of public presentations and teaching that can last all day. Through my journaling, I found that I drank four or five diet sodas per day to keep me caffeinated and "up" for the presentations. I was completely unaware of this bad habit; I thought I probably drank one during the day.

I weaned myself off the sodas over the course of a month. Now I have one cup of coffee in the morning and stay away from the soda habit. I didn't lose a whole of weight, but I did become aware of the negative habit. I do food journaling once every other month to stay aware of my eating habits.

What's a keystone habit you can begin to develop that would have a huge impact on your life—meditation, exercise, eating three healthy meals a day, cutting down on drinking? Focus on one and see what the ripple effects are.

A Summary Point

It's easy to start big and get overwhelmed quickly by lack of progress or accomplishment. Procrastinators tend to be overly aspirational and ambitious when forming a new habit.

Let's say you want to get into better physical condition. You tell yourself, "I will start running three miles a day." Although it's a positive habit to develop, running that far will be a challenging start, especially if you are out of shape.

There are a number of writers (Clear, 2018; Guise, 2013) who talk about developing "tiny" or "mini" habits to avoid biting off more than we can chew. They believe that if we start off small, sometimes *very* small, over time we can build a great habit.

In the example of running, they would suggest you consider *walking* a quarter of a mile on the first day, which is rather easy and accomplishable and therefore a good beginning of a mini habit. Walk a quarter of a mile each day for a week, and after seven days you will have walked 1.75 miles, which is a nice achievement.

In the second week, walk half a mile daily. At the end of the week, you will have walked 3.5 miles, which is a 100% improvement in a week.

In week three, run—*slowly*—a quarter of a mile each day and walk the other quarter of a mile. (If you feel you can actually run half a mile a day, then do so, but be careful.) Do the same math as in weeks one and two. At the end of week three, you will have run 1.75 miles and walked the same distance.

In week four, run half a mile each day. By the end of the week, you will have run 3.5 miles, hopefully injury-free.

You can continue the same careful process, and in another month or so, you will be running 3.5 miles daily, which would be a great accomplishment. The key here is that small steps, over time, can reap huge benefits.

Many procrastinators fail to realize that *smallness* is the key to success. We tend to be impatient with this pace. If we can keep our eye on the prize and develop some patience, over time we can accomplish great things.

To push the point a little further, for writers, producing written pages is the primary goal. I will talk more later about a famous author who wrote over sixty books and gave this advice: "I try and write 2 crappy pages a day." This is a great mini habit that will produce 60 pages a month and a 300-page book in six months.

Note that he didn't say two great pages every day but two "crappy" ones. Once you have three hundred pages of rough draft, you can get them edited by a professional and have a book to sell. I have followed this process for my last two books, and it has worked well for me.

Elsewhere in this book, I talk about separating writing from editing. These are two very different processes. If you try to do both as you write, there is a good chance you will get frustrated and even procrastinate about writing.

Go small to go big *eventually*, rather than starting big and ending up small.

Lever 2: The Myths and Realities of Willpower

I can resist anything but temptation.
—Oscar Wilde

The notion of willpower has been around for a long time and dates to the Victorian era. People then were quite afraid that some people could not control their urges and impulses, like drinking, swearing, overeating, and laziness. They focused on self-control and willpower as ways to control these unnatural desires and appetites. Many of these ideas have survived in our modern era and influence much of the thinking about willpower.

Some definitions:

- Merriam Webster: "the ability to *control* yourself, strong determination that allows you to do something difficult such as lose weight, quit smoking

- Dictionary.com: *control* of one's *impulses* and action, self-control.

- Cambridge Dictionary: the ability to *control* your own thoughts and the way in which you behave.

- MacMillan Dictionary: The ability to *control* your thoughts and behavior in order to achieve something

I've always had big questions about willpower all my life. I think there is a lot of mythology about it, and most of those myths are not very helpful. We have been taught that we need to be "strong," to tough it out. We need to be more disciplined. We need to suck it up. And still many people struggle with addictions, often for their entire lives. Do all these people lack willpower? Are they just weak or lazy? I don't think so.

I strongly believe that too many people beat themselves up for not having "enough" willpower. They believe they are weak individuals. This self-criticism isn't helpful (Pyschl, 2013; Fiore, 2007). Yet many people persist in this thinking and just feel bad about themselves. Procrastinators often feel guilty about their habit and wish, "If only I had the willpower to break this habit."

When we look at the mean habit of procrastination, is willpower the answer to our problems? I am not sure about this. In the next few pages, I am going to unpack some of the research about willpower so we better understand its complexity and can use it effectively.

The study of willpower was greatly influenced by Walter Mischel, a Stanford University psychologist who conducted a series of experiments with young children (3–5 years old). In his famous study, children were offered a choice between one small but immediate reward—a marshmallow—or two marshmallows if they waited about fifteen minutes. The researchers explained the rules to the children and then left the room as the children were videotaped. (*Procrastination note*: You can view the videos on YouTube by looking up "Stanford Marshmallow Test.")

In follow-up studies, the researchers found that the children who were able to wait longer and get two marshmallows tended to have better life outcomes (e.g., higher SAT scores, higher educational attainment, healthier lifestyles). The children's ability to delay gratification—in other words, exercise willpower—correlated with positive future outcomes.

Subsequent experiments uncovered different outcomes and indicated that the children's home environment, family background, and early cognitive ability were important influences.

Michell's experiment is one of the most famous ones in the field of psychology and, in my view, overly influenced the study of willpower for decades. When you are 3–5 years old, does your ability to exert self-control define your future? I am not sure about this. As future experiments are conducted, we will learn more about what actually influences the complex notion of willpower.

Let's be cognizant that many of these experiments were conducted in a laboratory setting, not in the real world of school, home, and playground. Kelly McGonigal (2013), another expert on willpower, has also questioned the implications of these "artificial" studies.

Roy F. Baumeister (2011) is one of the giants in the field of willpower. His book with John Tierney, *Willpower: Rediscovering the Greatest Human Strength* is one of the most-read books about this subject. He coined the term "ego depletion" and sees willpower as a muscle that can be developed over time. If you exercise your willpower too much, it can also get worn out.

He conducted many studies to understand the complexity of willpower and discovered that after people exerted self-control on one task, their willpower was depleted for other tasks. It seemed that people lost energy or a resource of some kind after exercising self-control. In fact, he found that using willpower feels physically exhausting.

For Baumeister and others (Johnson, 2016; Duhigg, 2012) it is important to set fewer clear goals and make sure they are compatible with each other. For example, if you want to make and eat dinner with your family every night, going to graduate school in the evening might not work.

You don't have different willpower "buckets" for work, exercise, watching what you eat, and so on—it all comes from one *limited* bucket. The lesson here is not to work on several things at once, like losing weight *and* writing a book *and* learning a language. That's probably way too much to tackle at one time. Remember, small can be beautiful.

Baumeister and others suggest that it's important to see the connection between what you are doing (and probably procrastinating about) and your long-term goals and purposes. How can what you are doing currently bring you closer to your higher aspirations? Having a clear vision for yourself in the future can be a powerful motivator to do what needs to be done today. This theme of having a meaningful purpose is a consistent idea in the procrastination research and something every procrastinator should think about.

Baumeister makes some thoughtful recommendations to consider.

- Don't overschedule yourself. It can be overwhelming and can deplete your willpower. Too many managers and leaders have way too many meetings piled one right after another, and they are exhausted by the end of the day. Try not cramming your schedule to the brim. Don't feel self-important because your schedule is always full.

- The amount of available willpower declines as you use it, especially in decision-making. He counsels that we should make important decisions early in the day, because we might not be as alert or decisive later in the afternoon. He cites research about Israeli parole boards: before lunch, they made many decisions in favor of the parole candidates (80% in fact), but later in the afternoon, as they tired, only 20% of the decisions were in favor of the candidates—something to seriously think about.

- In one of Baumeister's experiments, students who were forced to meticulously plan their day found that their grades suffered more than the students who set weekly or monthly goals. Too much specificity isn't helpful.

Kelly Mc Gonigal's (2013) book *The Willpower Instinct* brings another perspective to the table. She questions much of the research on willpower because many of the experiments have been conducted under laboratory or highly structured conditions. Although I tend to agree with her position, we still need to be respectful and thoughtful about what we have learned so far from those experiments.

Mc Gonigal believes we can build our willpower if we make choices consistent with our highest goals and highest values, even when some part of us doesn't want to do the hard things. In her view, we need to identify our highest purposes and align our actions with them.

Once again, although I agree with her perspective, I believe that having clear purposes and goals simply isn't enough. That's why I wrote this book. It's not that simple, in my view. We need a range of effective strategies, practices, protocols, and even hacks to get ourselves aligned with our values and purposes.

Like other researchers (Duhigg, 2014; Clear, 2018), Mc Gonigal talks about the importance of mindfulness and notes that small changes over time can make a real difference.

She discusses the notion observed by neuroscientists that self-control resides in an area of the brain called the *prefrontal cortex*. Each time we use the prefrontal cortex to make decisions, resist temptations, and think through difficult problems, we deplete our limited willpower. This is consistent with Baumeister's findings and is aligned with other researchers in the field. She cautions that if we are not careful, we will use up this limited resource, which can lead to excessive procrastination. She makes some recommendations about building our willpower reserve:

- Become aware of shallow breathing, and slow your breathing down to 4–5 breaths per minute.

- Forgive yourself. This is important to her because she believes people can be too self-critical.

- Practice meditation and get enough sleep and exercise.

One of Mc Gonigal's most interesting notions is about having a clear picture of your future self, and how that influences procrastination big-time. For most of us, our future self is a stranger. We don't see the connection between what we do currently and our future well-being.

She recommends that we need to create a "future memory" of ourselves by imagining the life we would like to have in the future. If we see ourselves as people who exercise regularly, save money for retirement, eat healthily, and sleep well, it can help create a higher aspiration that will enable us to do the difficult things necessary to achieve our preferred future.

One of the techniques she employs is to have her students write a letter to themselves from the perspective of looking back from a point several years from now and describing what they see. Again, this picture of a future self can be a powerful motivator.

There are divergent views about willpower. I want to share a different perspective so we have a fuller understanding. Amy Johnson (2016), in her book *Little Book of Change*, doesn't believe that willpower is an effective tool for overcoming bad habits. She thinks that when you attempt to use willpower to overcome an urge, you end up thinking about that urge even more and creating a stronger neural pathway for that habit.

She prefers that we be aware of our urges and see them as passing thoughts. She suggests that we slow down our breathing and practice mindfulness and self-compassion. The author has a spiritual bent to her thinking, and many people might be attracted to the way she sees things.

She notes that setbacks are not uncommon—a resonant theme throughout this book—and that we can bounce back from them. We can develop resilience with patience and practice. She suggests that we set clear goals and track progress so that we can experience it. She also cautions that we often have too many goals, so we need to reduce the number and complexity of them. Remember that procrastinators tend to be overly ambitious and aspirational. Her advice should be seriously considered.

Although I am not particularly attracted to Johnson's spiritual focus, she has some useful and practical ideas that are strongly aligned with the research on managing procrastination.

Benjamin Hardy (2018) wrote *Willpower Doesn't Work* and provides another contrary view about willpower. He suggests that we fail to realize the powerful influence that our physical environments have on us and the accomplishment of our goals. He wants us to intentionally *design* our environments so that they are distraction-free. I agree with this notion—but, once again, it's simply not enough.

His strongest recommendation is to create separate spaces for work and play. This is much easier said than done, given that the COVID-19 pandemic has forced millions of people to be at home while still working. I have been a remote worker for over thirty years, and I have always had a home office in a separate part of my house. For the most part, the separation works pretty well. But it still can be difficult even after all these years, because many temptations are lurking 15 feet away.

Hardy doesn't want us to rely on willpower. He suggests practices like implementation intentions and specific rituals that can neutralize our procrastination tendencies.

I don't believe it's an either/or proposition. I believe that designing your physical environment (e.g., decreasing clutter, making quiet space, turning off notifications) is a good and practical idea if you can pull it off. In addition, you still need all the help you can get with procrastination. The many strategies in this book need to be considered and utilized.

Willpower Hacks

Baumeister suggests that when we feel our willpower is tapped out, we should just eat something. Protein is better than something sugary because sugar will only give you a temporary boost. Eat something healthy and see what happens.

Duhigg (2012) and McGonnial (2013) both suggest that having a support group can be very helpful in enhancing your willpower. Groups like Alcoholics Anonymous and Weight Watchers have been around for years. Also, consider joining a running or walking group to help motivate you to improve your health. Authors often join writers' groups to get the support they need from colleagues.

Following a specific routine, such as laying out work clothes the night or eating an easy-to-prepare, healthy breakfast every morning, can be helpful because a routine neutralizes the need to decide or to rely on your willpower to tough it out.

Stress depletes willpower dramatically. So, when you feel stressed, do something to relieve it. Take a walk, exercise, meditate for 10 minutes, do some deep breathing, ask others for help, watch nature—whatever positive activity you can engage in to relieve your stress.

Remove the temptation if you can. This can range from putting your phone in another room to not driving by a casino. Just don't put yourself in a position to be tempted. This is not easy to do sometimes, but it can be an effective strategy. For many years I have not had any ice cream in my freezer because I love ice cream, which has millions of calories. That one practice has helped me maintain my weight. Otherwise I would eat several pints of Ben & Jerry's each week and wonder how all the pounds jumped on me.

Try to do important things early in the day if you are a morning person. We lose willpower throughout the day. Be sure you don't make important decisions—unless you have to—late in the day. For those people who experience their "power hour" later in the day, use the same strategy. Focus your attention and willpower at the times you feel strongest and most alert.

Remember: we are *not* weak or lazy. Get rid of that kind of thinking and self-talk. It just isn't helpful.

This Is My Takeaway about Willpower

I tend to agree with the metaphors of willpower being like a battery or a muscle with limited energy. If you agree with this thinking, then you have to be very strategic about how and when you use your willpower.

- When you start a new habit, use many of the strategies in the book (e.g., chewable chunks, really small goals, temptation bundling) and rely on your willpower as you start your new habits. Don't expect to punch through your habit; you will tire quickly, and you want to avoid this.

- I like the idea that willpower is like a muscle and can be built over time. This gives me hope that I can gradually improve my willpower. But it is still a limited resource. Use it strategically, not for the long haul.

- I hate the notion that many of us, especially procrastinators, lack willpower and aren't strong enough to do what needs to be done. I think that in some areas of my life, I have exceptional willpower—and in other areas, not so much. I suspect that describes most people. What I strive to do and want to be better at is having fewer, realistic, but aspirational goals and using the limited resource of willpower to

  - start a project and create some momentum

  - close the last mile on a project

Lever 3: Focus and Attention

> The man who chases two rabbits, catches neither.
> —Confucius

I want to briefly review a few books about focus and attention to lay the groundwork for these important ideas. If we can't learn to gradually focus our attention and manage our distractions, we will never be able to deal effectively with our procrastination habit—never.

We live in an extraordinarily distractible society, full of smartphones, emails, Twitter, Facebook, WhatsApp, newspapers, and so on. It is difficult to focus your attention on your most important work with distractions everywhere. This will not change in the future; in fact, the pace and complexity we face will only increase. We need to learn how to manage our attention if we are going to accomplish what matters.

One of the big challenges is that we are naturally drawn to urgent tasks. An unanticipated phone call, a request for a surprise meeting, or an email marked "high priority" is attractive and addictive.

Daniel Goleman (2014) is one of the most famous and prolific psychological researchers in the last 30 years. He made the term "emotional intelligence" part of leadership vernacular throughout the world. His book *Focus: The Hidden Driver of Excellence* is a useful resource for us to consider as we attempt to manage our procrastination habit. If we can learn to focus our attention, we can be more productive and even happier people.

Goleman introduced the term "smart practice," which entails meditation, mindfulness, focused preparation, recovery from setbacks, understanding of the learning curve, and the use of positive emotions to improve our performance.

Goleman and others (Clear, 2018; Newport, 2016) compare attention to a muscle you can strengthen and flex. This is very similar to Baumeister's notions about willpower. He discusses the power and effectiveness of "selective attention," which is the ability to focus on *one* task, despite all the sensory and emotional distractions present in our lives.

Goleman proposes the "triad of attention," which consists of (a) inner attention, (b) outer attention, and (c) other attention. Inner attention is the ability to pay attention to your gut feelings, intuition, values, and decision-making abilities. Outer attention allows us to navigate the outside world effectively. Other attention pertains to how we relate to and connect with other people.

We need to develop all three types of attention to be effective, productive, and fulfilled. Once again, we see the theme of the interrelatedness of things. Most important ideas are not isolated from each other, but are part of a tapestry of interconnectedness.

Goleman provides some advice that can help us build our attention. He believes taking breaks can be helpful. Meditation helps build focus. Things like exercise, walking in nature, and doing fun things all help build our attentional capacity. He also notes that when we are doing something we enjoy, it's quite easy to focus on it. Conversely, when we face a difficult task, our emotions often intrude (e.g., anger, frustration, anxiety), and the task becomes more difficult.

This is common sense, but procrastinators often let our emotional state dictate our actions. We can learn—with practice and over time—to manage the negativity of our emotions and understand how they can influence our actions.

Goleman's final piece of advice is that the more we can focus on the priority things, the more our performance and emotional state will improve. His thinking is aligned with that of other researchers. They also talk about the importance of self-reflection, taking time to just think, and allowing for intentional wandering time, when we can be creative and discover new ideas.

The good news is that attention can be developed with use, practice, and exercise. It's one of the most powerful levers we have for achieving a good life.

Goleman cautions us that just selecting the right things isn't enough. We also have to say no to the wrong things. In chapter 6, the mini chapter section, I share some effective ways to say no to requests in a collegial and strategic way.

In David Lakhani's (2006) book, *The Power of an Hour*, he talks about developing "fearsome focus." This is where you strive to create a one-hour time slot during which you focus on your most important task. At first glance, one hour of focused time might not seem like a lot. But it can be very productive.

You will probably need to build your focused attention in 15-minute increments over time and try not to tackle a whole hour at first. As I have mentioned before, procrastinators are often overly optimistic and aspirational about what they can actually accomplish. So it's important to manage your expectations and build your attention capacity over time.

Make sure that you take a 10–15 minute break after every hour of focused time. Strive mightily *not* to engage in social media during your break. It can take you down a rabbit trail quickly, and you will find yourself getting distracted by all the "interesting" things. Take a walk, read something interesting, or chat with a friend, but stay away from social media.

You might have to negotiate with your boss, coworkers, or partner to agree on this "sacred hour." Ideally, you are not available during this stated time unless there is an emergency. Conversely, you might have to negotiate with your colleagues about their own sacred hour and be supportive of their efforts.

Mini Case Study

I have worked with several clients over the past two years who implemented a sacred hour for each day of their work week. It was a game changer. Their people found that with just one hour, they were very productive. Their HR departments anonymously assessed the effectiveness of this one strategy and found that over 90% of participants wanted to keep this protected time because it was so productive. Note that they didn't ask for more protected time, which seems like a natural thing to want. One hour was plenty of time to focus on their priorities.

A caution: Just because you have a sacred hour in your life doesn't guarantee that you won't procrastinate during it. You might have to use many of the techniques and tactics suggested in the book to neutralize your tendency to procrastinate during this time. You will probably have to build your focused attention over time.

I have found that I can only focus for 30 minutes at a time. I have tried to build up to an hour, but it doesn't work for me. After every 30-minute work slot, I take a 10-minute break.

The Why

Many of the researchers who study focus and attention discuss the important notion of finding the purpose or the why of your work. They suggest that if we have passion for the task (e.g., writing a book, creating a garden, decorating a house, starting a nonprofit), our why can help us stay focused. McGonigal (2013) talks about serving a purpose bigger than yourself as a major factor in accomplishing things.

Unfortunately, many of the projects, tasks, and assignments we are responsible for don't have deep meaning and purpose. We still have to do them anyway. If you can see the connection between the mundane tasks and your most important goals, it will enhance your motivation to work on them. It probably won't make them any easier, but the suffering will have some meaning because you are serving a higher purpose or goal.

That's why I share scores of practices and protocols to use when the tasks *aren't* exciting, enjoyable, or wonderful. In some ways they help you get over the hump because you need to accomplish them regardless of how you feel about them.

A Different Perspective on Attention and Distraction

Nir Eyal in his book *Indistractable: How to Control Your Attention and Choose Your Life* (2019) presents some dramatically different ideas about attention and distraction. Although I don't agree with some of his ideas, I want to share his thinking because procrastinators need as many different perspectives and approaches as they can get in dealing with this habit.

Eyal shares the powerful and sad findings of a research project conducted in 2014 and reported in the respected journal *Science.* In this experiment, researchers asked participants to sit in a room and think for 15 minutes. The room was empty except for a device that allowed subjects to give themselves a mild but painful electric shock.

When asked beforehand, every participant in the study said that they would pay to avoid getting an electronic shock. However, when left alone in the room with the electronic shock machine and nothing else to do, 67% of the men and 25% of the women gave themselves an electronic shock. Many of them shocked themselves *several* times.

I realize this is a dramatic example, but it does point out something important. Many of us have a hard time just being with ourselves. Most of us will have to build up our tolerance for being alone. If focusing on one thing and eliminating distractions are two of the most effective strategies in dealing productively with procrastination, this will be a real challenge for many people. So when I emphasize starting small and building capacity over time, I mean it. Bottom line, paying atten-tion and learning to focus take practice. They don't just happen.

The following are some more of Eyal's suggestions and recommendations, many of which are aligned with those of other researchers about procrastination. First, he uses the terms *distraction* and *traction* to explain his thinking. He defines distraction as actions that move us away from what we really want. Traction is actions that move us toward what we really want.

He sees distraction as coming from within, when we want to escape boredom or anxiety or other uncomfortable feelings. Eyal proposes that how we deal with our uncomfortable internal triggers and emotions determines whether we seek healthy acts of traction or self-defeating distraction. To master our internal triggers, we need to learn how to deal with discomfort. By observing our urges and allowing them to dissolve, we can reconfigure the triggers or the task. If we can develop mindfulness, the powerful urges we tend to respond to quickly become less potent over time. He suggests that we explore the negative sensations with curiosity instead of contempt and criticism.

To hack back your external triggers and defend your focus, send fewer emails, get out of group chats, and turn off notifications. This is a familiar theme mentioned throughout the book. He also cautions that we should be attentive and cautious during transitions, because they can create the opportunity to get distracted.

We should look for the emotions that precede the distraction (e.g., boredom, anxiety, fear) and write them down so that we better understand how distraction occurs and our internal reaction to those triggers.

To be more focused, turn you values into time by allocating and scheduling time for yourself and the important relationships in your life. Neil Fiore (2007), who I mentioned earlier, also suggests this strategy so that we have more balanced lives and avoid resenting our workloads. We need to schedule our personal time as well as our professional time and then adhere to the schedule.

Finally, Eyal is a big fan of precommitments that help to remove future choices. He identifies three kinds of precommitments:

- An *effort pact* makes unwanted behaviors difficult to do, such as using blocking apps to stay focused.

- A *price pact* involves assigning some cost, usually money, to getting distracted. In short, you pay a price for being distracted.

- An *identity pact* involves a practice about which you label yourself in a positive way, such as "I am a devout Muslim" or "I am a vegetarian," and adhere to that identity. A vegetarian won't be distracted by a meal decision that involves meat. A devout religious person will observe their religion's practices without being distracted by other temptations.

Some Recommendations

1. Focus on *one* thing at a time. Many authors talk about this habit (Goleman, 2014; Pressfield, 2012; Ferrari, 2010), and lot of procrastinators will find this challenging to accomplish. It is important to pick the right task at the right time and apply your thinking and attention to accomplish these important tasks.

Multitasking is a waste of time and one of the biggest procrastination habits that procrastinators fall into. Trying to do a couple of things at a time simply doesn't work; the research is strong about this reality. We tend to multitask because it makes us feel busy and occupied. I could cite thousands of studies about the negative habits of multitasking, but will only share two of the more striking ones.

"Multitasking and IQ: A Study at the University of London": Researchers found that participants who multitask during cognitive tasks experienced IQ score declines that were similar to what they would expect if they smoked marijuana or stayed up all night. IQ drops of 15 points for multitasking men lowered their scores to the average range for an 8-year-old!

And in the book *The Distracted Mind* (2016), Adam Gazzaley and Larry D. Rosen found that multitasking causes safety risks. Smartphone use while driving in particular increases risk. This inattention causes 23% of all US crashes! Many of us are driving, texting, and talking on our smartphones at the same time, even though it's deadly.

You get the point—multitasking is a powerful and negative myth that makes us stupid and can actually kill people. It isn't productive ever. Don't do it.

2. Make sure your physical surroundings support your focus. Again, this is a pervasive theme throughout this book. If your workspace is full of distractions, you are in trouble. It's as simple as that. Strive to do whatever you can to eliminate distractions. It will enable you to focus your attention strategically. *This will not be easy.*

3. Take mental breaks. If you find yourself wandering off mentally into distraction-land, take a short 10-minute break and do something else. Don't engage with social media because it will suck you in and absorb your attention.

I realize this will be challenging, but this one practice can prevent you from procrastinating. Take a walk, get some tea, do some stretching exercises, listen to music—just do something different. Often this break will create a shift in energy and thinking, and you might be able to get back on track.

4. Have a notepad next to you to capture your random thoughts. Instead of having all these ideas bouncing around your head, capture them in writing and put them aside. You can review them later, after you have finished your work period. Writing them down gets them out of your conscious mind temporarily and lets you refocus your attention.

David Allan (2015) has written a number of popular books about time management and productivity. He tells us that our brains have almost limitless storage space, but our attention is very limited. He also asserts that our brains are not for storing but for thinking. Get the clutter out of your head and onto paper.

I have a notepad on my desk at all times. When wandering thoughts, creative ideas, or reminders pop into my head, I quickly capture them and keep focusing on my work. At the end of the day, I usually review my notepad to see what I need to pay attention to. If there is something pressing, then I will look at it during one of my frequent breaks and respond if necessary. The key thing here is to capture it and keep moving forward. Do not take a rabbit trail downward.

5. We are drawn to urgent tasks like a strong magnet. An unanticipated phone call or an unexpected email can derail our focus and distract our attention quickly. Often these urgent tasks are created by someone else's problems, challenges, and priorities. People we work with are asking for help.

Urgent tasks can make us feel occupied, busy, productive, important, and needed. Unfortunately, they are rarely effective and enable our procrastination habit to kick in big time. They draw us away from our priorities to serve other people's priorities.

Do whatever you can to create and maintain your focus. Get rid of the "I should be able to focus" mindset. It simply isn't helpful. Maintaining focus is not easy due to our distractible environment. Sometimes you will have to change your physical environment to one that has minimal distractions *if* you can.

For example, when I have to do my writing, I often go the local library, which is a short walk from my home office. I find an out-of-the-way desk and start my work process. It is relatively quiet there from nine in the morning until three in the afternoon; after that, local students come in to "study" and the library becomes a distraction magnet. I leave at three and never try to fight those distractions.

There is also a university several miles from my house which has a rare thing: a quiet room. All the students who study there maintain silence. It's a pretty amazing place and a gift in my professional life. It's always good to have a plan B.

Lastly, whenever I start a new book or am struggling with finishing one, I rent a *cheap* motel room at the New Jersey Shore. I love the ocean and find it a place for renewal and relaxation. I wake up in the morning and walk for an hour on the beach. Then I write for several hours in 30-minute increments with 10-minute breaks in between. It's distraction-free because I only bring writing paper, my computer with no apps, and my smartphone, which I check early in the morning and again in the evening for important messages. It's a highly productive week for me and something I have done since I wrote my dissertation 30 years ago.

Bottom line, find a distraction-free place any way you can, even if it is only for a couple of hours, and you will find that you can be very productive.

Chris Bailey's book *Hyper-Focus* (2018) provides great advice on how to be more productive in a world of distraction. He talks about the notion of hyper-focus being a "superpower" that enables you to focus on one thing at a time .This will take some real practice for procrastinators. You don't become a great golfer because you buy an expensive set of golf clubs. You have to practice a lot. The same is true with focusing on one thing at a time.

Bailey, like other researchers, talks about the bad habit of multitasking, where we flit from task to task but don't accomplish very much. It might feel like we are being busy and therefore productive, but we aren't. The "switching costs" alone are very expensive in terms of time. Bailey notes that it can take up to 20 minutes to reorient ourselves to the task we started with. It can also take 50% longer to complete the task.

Bailey presents a powerful notion that he calls the "attention space." It describes "the amount of mental capacity we have available to focus and process things." Our attention space is what we are aware of at any given time. It's the scratch pad or clipboard of our brains that we use to temporally store information as it's being processed.

As with willpower, our attention space is pretty limited. Complex tasks that require our conscious engagement take up most of our attention space.

Bailey has some specific advice worth considering. Some of these ideas might feel repetitive, but there aren't hundreds of great strategies or ideas to combat procrastination. The fact that so many experts tend to converge on a handful of ideas is a positive thing in my view.

- Make your physical environment less distracting.

- Focus on no more than three priority tasks in a day. You might want to start with one priority task at first and build up to three.

- Use a chime or alarm of some kind periodically to check and see if you are focused, wandering, or distracted.

- Meditate, which helps with focus over time.

- Use headphones to completely block out distractions and noise. (I have tried this and didn't like it, but many of my colleagues use this tactic and find it helpful.)

- Understand your prime biological time and do your most important work during this period.

- Take numerous breaks throughout the day (my favorite!).

Caution: try one of these suggestions at a time. Don't overreach by trying three or four—it probably won't work

An Interesting Idea: Attention Residue

Attention residue happens when we leave a task unfinished and move on to another task. Our brains find it hard to let go of these uncompleted tasks. They live in the backs of our minds as we try to focus on something else. I call this the "shadow" of the previous task. It stay with us in the present. This residue can prevent us from focusing all our attention on the current task.

All of us have experienced a guilty feeling when we blow off a chore to go and have a little fun. We don't fully enjoy the fun activity because that little voice in our heads reminds us of what we left behind. Completing a step—if not the whole task—can help keep that voice at bay. Mark the moment of completing a step and then go and have some fun.

Lever 4: Mindfulness and Self-Compassion Are Keys to Managing Procrastination

Mindfulness refers to the practice of "paying attention to your attention." In short, it is bringing one's attention to experiences occurring in the present moment, without judgment. This judgment piece is the key, because we can be very critical in our thinking about almost everything.

Meditation is a wonderful way to manage our attention and sustain it over time. There are hundreds of books and thousands of articles about the practice of meditation—so many that it can be overwhelming. There is also some confusing mystique surround meditation, along with a sprinkling of spirituality about it. Later I will suggest a couple of great books about the topic, but for now I will share a simple explanation of how to meditate.

- Find a place where you won't get distracted.

- Find a comfortable chair that will help you focus your attention for about 10 minutes initially.

- Close your eyes.

- Focus on your breathing by breathing in slowly and deeply and then exhaling slowly. Take four to five deep breaths per minute.

- Your mind will wander. This is *normal*. Just notice your wandering mind without judgment and bring your attention back to your breathing.

Try to do ten minutes of meditation at first. Build up your practice over time until you are able to sit and meditate for twenty minutes.

Caution: Ten minutes might sound like a long time, and initially it might feel endless. You might get a little anxious, so be patient with the process. You might even start with five minutes to begin with, to build your capacity. This isn't a contest. Take your time and follow the process I have described.

Make sure you don't *over aspire,* which is a tendency for procrastinators. By this I mean don't try to do 30 minutes initially, because you will probably fail. Start small and build your mediation practice over time

So why learn to meditate?

Almost always when procrastinators begin to experience uncomfortable feelings as they contemplate a noxious task, they quickly avoid their feelings and the procrastination habit kicks into full gear. This avoidance results in putting off or delaying the task. It happens in seconds and is often unconscious. It's like a knee-jerk reaction that plays out over and over again.

But if you can learn to just pay attention to the feelings (mindfulness) and not act on them so quickly, you can create the possibility of stopping the procrastination process cold. This will not be easy and will take some practice, patience, and courage.

This is a key theme to consider: just because you have certain negative emotions doesn't mean that you have to *act* on them. Paying attention to them for 30–60 seconds can to create the psychological space needed to choose the next step rather than acting impulsively. You do not have to be a victim of or at the mercy of your thoughts and emotions.

Next time you feel the urge to procrastinate, watch your emotions and self-talk (e.g., *This project is way too hard* or *I don't think I can do this*) and try not to act (avoid). Pay attention to what is happening. Often you will find that the urge to avoid the task loses much of its power. It might not go away, but the strong feelings of stress and anxiety may be diminished enough that you don't have to act on them immediately.

You will have to be patient with this approach. Our thoughts and emotions can be powerful things, and we often react to them unconsciously. If you try to be nonjudgmental and stay in the moment, you can begin to neutralize their negative impact and your reactions.

If you can learn to meditate on a daily basis, you will find that your awareness increases and your reactivity decreases. Meditation is one of the most effective practices you can implement to help neutralize the procrastination habit.

Two books I recommend are *Practical Meditation for Beginners: 10 Days to a Happier, Calmer You* (2018) by Benjamin W. Decker; and

Meditation: How to Meditate: A Practical Guide to Making Friends with Your Mind (2013) by Thublen Chondron.

There is an interesting video on YouTube, "Building Awareness of the Procrastination Urge," by Leo Babauta. It provides some good advice on managing your procrastination. Here are a few of his tips.

- Track your impulses to procrastinate by using some kind of scoring or reminder system. He suggests that you create a daily log if you can. Review the log periodically to identify when you procrastinate (e.g., in the late afternoon, when you are tired), where you procrastinate (e.g., at work, at home, both), and what you procrastinate about (e.g., house chores, errands, writing a report).

- He suggests an interesting behavior modification technique: put a rubber band on one of your wrists, and whenever you get the urge to procrastinate, switch the band to the other wrist. This will physically and visually remind you of how often you procrastinate during the day.

- Ask yourself some questions to raise your awareness about your procrastination habit. For example,

  - What reason do I have for putting this task off?

  - Why do I feel it is so difficult to do?

  - How many times have I done something similar successfully?

  - What did I do then to get started?

  - What's the easiest step that I can take to get started right now?

Barbauta also encourages self-care. Ask yourself, "Do I feel tired?" If so, consider taking a nap, taking a walk, or meditating. Disconnect from the present task. He also suggests that you can make a small commitment to a friend. Lastly, he strongly suggests that you create a practice space where there are no distractions, and then focus on the task at hand. He has an interesting website, zenhabits.net, that is worth a look.

This leads to my next point: *self-compassion* is also vitally important, because most procrastinators are really hard on themselves. They beat themselves up psychologically and feel a lot of shame and guilt about their negative habit. This only feeds the procrastination cycle and doesn't help anything (Pychyl, 2013).

Forgive yourself for the procrastination. Try to apply one of the practices and protocols in this book and move forward. This is an important point: do not try to implement several new practices. That will be too many, and will feed the procrastination habit big-time. You will get overwhelmed by trying to do a lot of new things differently, and nothing will really work for you.

One small step can make a difference. For example, if you just go to a place without distractions for one or two hours a week, you might find that this works for you. Or shut the door to your office for a couple of hours a week, and see if you become more productive. Or reward yourself for accomplishing tasks for a week. See what happens with one of these practices, *not* many of them.

Many of my colleagues use fancy and expensive headphones when they are traveling on planes. They report they get real work done on their trips. What is usually lost time has turned into value-added time for them. Try this with a task that you have been putting off, and, once again, see what happens. There are over a hundred ideas in this book; pick one and try it.

Here's a final piece of advice: treat yourself like you would treat a very good friend, with care and kindness. We beat ourselves up way too much about our procrastination habit. It isn't helpful at all. Being kind to yourself is a strategic thing to do (Pychl, 2013; Fiore, 2007).

Chapter 3
21 Powerful Ideas about Managing Your Procrastination

1: Chewable Chunks Are the Way to Go

The problem most procrastinators have is getting *quickly* overwhelmed by the size, complexity and difficulty of the task or project they need to do. They often see the whole thing at once (e.g., write a long book; do all my taxes; paint the entire house) and then overestimate what it will take to complete the task (e.g., "It will take me forever!"). Hyperbolic overestimation creates stress very quickly, and the procrastination habit kicks into full gear. We will do almost anything to avoid the negative feelings that *we* create and avoid the task that needs to be done.

They key thing to remember is that almost all tasks have many smaller parts or steps to them. All you have to do—and this is not easy—is break the larger task into those smaller steps. This itself is an important task in the completion process, and one that procrastinators often forget.

The practice of breaking the larger task down into "chewable" parts is a huge step in the right direction. Give yourself credit for doing this and reward yourself with something nice for accomplishing this important first step. The chunks becomes an implementation road map that you can visually follow and see progress.

Then do one small step at a time. Don't try to tackle the whole thing, because you will start to procrastinate. For example, let's say you want to write a book, which is a large and complex task. For many people, it quickly becomes way too large to take on because they lose sight of the fact that books have *chapters*. Each chapter is an important step in the completion of the book. One chapter at a time is the key strategy to embrace, not writing the whole book all at once.

I have written many books. When I first started to write, my inner dialogue went like this: *My God, 250 pages, that's impossible. What am I going to say? Do I know enough? How am I going to write that much stuff? How much time will it take? I don't have all that time! I will need to do a whole lot of research so the book is informative and solid. That's really hard, reading and learning. What kind of research should I do? How much? What sources do I need to investigate? How will I know when I have enough? I am not good at editing my own work, so I will need someone to do that for me. How do I find someone who is good? Will I like working with them? How much will it cost? Will they be slow in returning my chapters? Will they be too critical? How will it slow down my writing? I have never published a book before. How does that work? Where do I find a publisher? Do I need an agent? Where do I find one? What if I write the book and no one wants to publish it? Then I have wasted hundreds of hours of my life! My God, I can't write a book!*

You get the idea. My inner monologue was nutty and all over the place. The enormity of the project overwhelmed me because I was thinking about *everything all at once*. I delayed writing my first book for a year because I didn't break the book into a series of smaller tasks. I kept thinking about how hard it would be to write a whole book.

This is how I got started: I sat with a colleague and talked through all the things that were overwhelming for me. She took extensive notes about all the blocks and hurdles I imagined. In an hour or so, she had 10 pages of notes, and we went to eat a nice lunch. We didn't talk about the book at lunch, to create some psychological space for me. After lunch, we began to organize the notes into a rough draft of a game plan for the book, identifying the barriers I needed to think about and some possible next steps. We used a flip chart (one of my favorite tools) to visually depict the challenges or "mud pies" along with some strategies to deal with the barriers we identified.

We then had a map of the territory I had to think about, and she helped me prioritize the next steps. This was a huge step in the whole process and helped me to move forward rather than let my procrastination habit kick in big-time.

A couple of notes here:

- I solicited the help of a trusted colleague and didn't get caught into the trap of doing everything myself. I got help. Remember this always: getting help is a very smart thing to do.

- We worked for an hour, *not* several hours. One hour is a chewable chunk.

- Then we went to lunch, which is a nice reward for a completed task. We did not talk about the task.

- After lunch, we returned to the task of organizing the notes—again, together, not me by myself.

- We created a rough draft, not a perfect outline. We drafted for an hour (another chewable chunk) and I had my game plan going forward.

Always try to break a bigger task into a set of smaller steps. It will help you manage the stress that usually kicks in with procrastinators and starts the procrastination habit churning into high gear almost immediately. Chewable chunks are the way to go.

Remember: focus on the next step, not the next thousand steps.

> The secret of getting ahead is getting started. The secret of getting started is breaking your complex, overwhelming tasks into smaller, manageable tasks and then starting on the first one.
>
> —Mark Twain

Procrastination Note

There is an outstanding TED Talk by Tim Urban, "Inside the Mind of a Master Procrastinator." He captures the essence of the procrastination habit in a funny, honest, and creative way. It's worth a look. I suggest that you see it with a friend and discuss its implications. It's great!

2. You Don't Do Your Best Work under Pressure

This is one of the most pervasive myths procrastinators believe; it's also a destructive one (Pychyl, 2013). Somehow, procrastinators have convinced themselves that if they wait until the last minute, the tremendous pressure that is created can help them produce their best work. Unfortunately, this is not true. There is no research that shows this approach is effective (Steel, 2007).

There might have been a time in the distant past where you did pull off a project—maybe cramming for an exam or writing a paper the night before it was due—and that memory has become an oversize legend in your mind.

But there are several reasons for *not* waiting until the last minute.

- The shadow of the project almost always looms large in your mind. You know you should get to it, but other things—usually enjoyable things—get in the way. This unfinished business is always present in the back of your mind and casts a shadow across your daily activities.

- You live with a lot of guilt and anxiety before you start the assignment, and the sprint to the end is full of stress and emotional strain. Is the project worth all that? Really? I understand the adrenaline rush we often experience in the dash at the end, but we pay a price for it. And it reinforces our procrastination habit big-time.

- When you wait until the last minute, you don't have any time to polish and refine your work. This could be a report that just doesn't get edited properly, and the mistakes and omissions cost you. It could be a hastily completed tax return that misses some helpful deductions.

Remember this notion, because it is an important one: we self-sabotage with this myth about the last minute sprint. It simply isn't true. In the long run, we pay a heavy price for this silly story we tell ourselves. Don't do it.

3. Rewards Work, so Use Them!

There is a fair amount of research that indicates that rewards can be helpful in managing procrastination. I know they work for me. The problem many procrastinators have is that they tell themselves that they "shouldn't" need to reward themselves to get something done. They should be mature enough to do the onerous task. This "shouldn't" thinking is very destructive and keeps the procrastination habit in full gear.

When you complete an important step in a large project, it's beneficial to give yourself a nice reward. I do not mean rewarding yourself after *every* little task, just the ones that matter (e.g., paying bills, writing a draft of a proposal, finishing income taxes). If you can come up with a variety of rewards and change them up, you will find that rewards can be helpful for several reasons.

- They mark the moment by acknowledging the accomplishment. This is very important psychologically because it feels like you are making progress and being successful.

- The anticipation of the reward can be motivating and help you push through to the end. In fact there is some research that indicates that the anticipation of the reward can be almost as exciting as the actual reward (Duhigg, 2012). So why wouldn't you do this for yourself? It's a double win, so do it.

- It can create some positive momentum going forward because the accomplishment *along with* the reward feels good and creates a positive memory. It builds implementation muscles and enables you to continue. Rewards plus accomplishments is a powerful combination in the execution journey.

We talked earlier about chewable chunks becoming a road map for a project. You can also create a reward map and think about the various ways you can reward yourself after the completion of a chewable chunk. Reward variety is the key to sustaining momentum, and it helps make the journey interesting and memorable.

Please get rid of the "shouldn't"—it's a motivation killer and simply not useful.

4. Starting Is Often the Hardest Part, so Make Starting as Easy as Possible

This is one of the most powerful notions to help you think about procrastination. For most procrastinators, starting is the hardest part, so the key is to make starting as easy as possible, however you can. The cure to procrastination is to move to action in spite of resistance, negative feelings, or stress. Movement creates momentum, and this can generate a feeling of accomplishment—you have actually gotten something done

The point to remember is that you don't have to do everything, which feels overwhelming. *Just do the next step*. Here are some examples of how:

- Write your to-do list late in the afternoon or the night before. It gives you a way of starting the next day quickly and without making any real decisions, which can generate confusion, doubt, and hesitation. Your list is waiting for you like a gift— do the first item on the list. Obviously it will take some discipline to start this organizing habit, but if you can do it for a week, and then assess whether it works for you, it's a great one to begin with.

- If you know you have a specific action to do in the morning— say, for example, exercise—lay out the necessary gear the night before. That way, when you wake up, everything you need is available *immediately*. Once again, no real thinking required— grab and go.

There is a famous story about the world-renowned dancer Twyla Tharp, who described her daily practice of exercising and dancing for many hours every day. When most people think about that kind of intense workout, they give up quickly. But she had all her dance stuff organized on her bed the night before, so that all she had to do when she woke up was grab and go. She took a cab and got to her workplace fast—no breakfast, chores, or grabbing a latte.

This might be an over-the-top example, given she was a world-class dancer, but her practice can be helpful to any of us in modified form. The keys are to make the task somewhat mindless and then to start it quickly so all the procrastination stuff—the decision-making, the hesitating, the overthinking—doesn't get a chance to kick in.

5. Waiting to Be "Inspired" Is Simply Foolish

This is one of the greatest whoppers of all time and one of the most pervasive myths procrastinators believe in. We wait until we "feel like it" or are "motivated" or are "inspired" to do the things we are procrastinating on. Unfortunately, the right time rarely comes, and the task remains unfinished.

Guess what? You may never feel like doing an unpleasant task—*never*. Quit fooling yourself. You have to deal with the uncomfortable feelings you experience and do the task anyway. Waiting to feel inspired is a fool's game and you know it.

Remember that our thoughts and emotions do not have to dictate our behavior. This is one of the most important principles regarding procrastination. You are not your emotions. You can push through and accomplish a task *without* positive feelings. You need to do it despite the negative emotions you may be experiencing or the silly self-talk I described earlier.

The kissing cousin of this myth is "I will feel more like doing it later." Again, this is baloney. You fool yourself in the moment, but you know that this is almost always not true.

Who waits until circumstances completely favor his undertaking will never accomplish anything.
—Martin Luther King

You can't get much done in life, if you only work on the days
when you feel good.
—Jerry West

The quotations above are from highly accomplished individuals who had to do a great deal of uncomfortable stuff during their whole lives. This is the key theme: there is a whole lot of difficult and uncomfortable stuff to do in life, so get on with it. Waiting for an onerous task to somehow become wonderful prevents you from tackling the task.

The task is always there, waiting to be done. Please use some of the ideas in this book to get started on completing them—whether you feel like it or not. You don't have to be at the mercy of your feelings all the time.

6. Procrastination Is Mostly Not a Time Management Problem—It's an Emotion Management Problem

This myth causes a lot of problems for a procrastinator because they believe that if they just use the right time management technique, they will be able to deal with their procrastination habit. Time management techniques can be very helpful, and I will share lots of them in this book. But procrastination is primarily a *self-management* problem at its core. If we can't manage the strong emotions and thoughts we have, then all the time management techniques in the world simply won't be very helpful.

I share several emotion management techniques throughout this book, like self-compassion, meditation, mindfulness, and visualization. All can be helpful when dealing with the emotional part of procrastination. If you don't deal with the emotional component of procrastination, then you are only skimming the surface.

The big lesson here is that you don't have to be a victim of your emotions. Just because you feel stress, anxiety, or overwhelm doesn't mean that you have to act on it, which usually means avoiding the task at hand. You can have negative feelings and *still act*. It isn't easy to do, but it is an essential and constructive behavior that can break the procrastination cycle. The way out of the cycle is through it.

7. Perfection Is an Expensive Habit and Generates a Whole Lot of Procrastination

Perfectionists almost always have an "all or nothing" mindset. Something is either perfect or it's a failure. The problem with this is that nothing is ever perfect. So the journey toward perfection is a tough slog with no real pleasure or satisfaction.

The tendency toward perfectionism feeds the procrastination habit. Perfectionists put extraordinary expectations on themselves. Then they think, *Nothing is good enough, so why start?* Even when perfectionists have done very well, they rarely experience a feeling of victory or accomplishment.

This is really true when perfectionists attempt something new or different, because a host of fears kick in: *Can I be excellent at this task? Will I be able to live up to my high standards? What if I make a mistake?* Given these fears, they will often put off the task until they think they can do it perfectly—which is almost never.

Perfectionists suffer a lot from social anxiety, worry, and depression. They often avoid new experiences because of a fear of failure and prefer to work alone. Many are poor delegators because they don't trust that other people can do the job to their high standards (Martin & Swinson, 2009; Smith, 2013).

I strongly believe that perfectionists need to deal directly with their perfectionism, because their procrastination habit is more of a symptom of their perfectionism. Although they have some similarities with us regular procrastinators, their perfectionism is the underlying and pervasive cause of their procrastination. They need to deal with this dynamic first.

Therapy and counseling can be helpful. This is not meant as a judgment of any kind, just a helpful suggestion to consider. Dealing with the powerful underlying causes of perfectionism can help mitigate the tendency to procrastinate.

Procrastinators/Perfectioners Note

There is an excellent book, *When Perfect Isn't Good Enough* (2009) by Martin M. Anthony and Richard P. Swinson, that people who tend to be perfectionists should read. It provides effective strategies and coping skills that help manage this powerful habit

One final note: don't be fooled by the popular notion that perfectionism is a "search for excellence" that drives the perfectionists—and isn't excellence a positive thing? Perfection is unattainable, in my view. Excellence is attainable with great effort and discipline. Let's make sure we are striving for something that is possible, not something extraordinary and unreachable.

What makes perfectionism so mean is that *everything* has to be at a very high standard. If you can, try to prioritize the most important things you want to accomplish, and apply your perfectionism to only those things. The secondary stuff doesn't need to be at the same level of excellence as the top priority stuff. This way you get to keep your habit, but let go of some of it with regard to the less important things in your life.

This isn't easy—I get that. But if you want to improve the quality of your life, thinking about how and where to apply your perfectionism is something to consider.

Mini Case Study

I had a client who was the CEO of a large, complex company, and he was a perfectionist. He worked with a therapist for several years and learned to differentiate between the number-one priorities for the company and the "nice to have" priorities. He applied his perfectionism to the number ones and was able to delegate the secondary priorities to his executive team. This freed up the decision-making process tremendously. It took some time and was not easy for him, but it worked. He also discovered that his executive team was very talented, which was an added bonus.

8. Your Environment Is Almost Always Distracting

Many chronic procrastinators have stimulating environments that are terribly distracting. For example, there's the messy desk, one of my constant failings. I tell myself that "I need to see everything I am working on," and it becomes a wonderful and destructive excuse for allowing clutter everywhere in my office.

How about instant email notifications? These are usually accompanied by a ring or ding or ping of some kind. Focus is immediately derailed. Who can resist the thought, *There is something new and exciting waiting for me!*

Then there's easy access to social media, where you can check in with others about your day, share what you are thinking, gossip, listen to breaking news, and watch the stock market.

In any busy, hectic, and noisy workplace where people are moving around and talking, there are lots of interruptions. It's a smorgasbord of distractions, and you can take advantage of myriad entertainments. It's the procrastinators' paradise and the death of productivity.

Procrastinators need to create a *productive* work environment, not a stimulating one. This is a powerful point—you have to minimize the distractions as much as you can. "Proximity to a temptation is one of the deadliest determinants of procrastination—the more enticing the distraction the less work we do" (Steel, 2007).

Some Strategies to Declutter Your Work Environment

A messy desk is a big distraction because the visual disorganization gets in the way. Looking for a missing paper, report, or file can exasperate you, and then the procrastination habit kicks into gear fast. We get frustrated because we have told ourselves, "I know where everything is on my sloppy desk." This is almost never true, but we persist with the myth.

You can use the time management technique of clearing up your desk by quarters. Tackle one quarter of the desk at a time. This takes time, attention, and discipline, but it will improve your productivity tremendously. It usually takes about an hour to clean and organize one quarter of your cluttered desk. Remember: take it in chewable chunks and reward yourself for each completed quarter.

If that doesn't work for you, then go someplace else—another office, the conference room, a library—and do not take any devices with you—just you, your computer, and relevant materials to get the task done. If you can go someplace else that doesn't have any distractions, you can get real work done.

Once again, do not succumb to the myth that you "shouldn't" need to go somewhere else to do your work. That's silly self-talk, which is also a distraction. If it works, do it. Find a quiet place or two.

Another suggestion to try is to put the phone away for one-hour time slots. Its constant companionship can be very distracting. We constantly check it for messages, troll social media, text our friends, and stay connected. This will not be easy to do, but it will neutralize your environmental distractions big-time. Remember to reward yourself after these one-hour time slots.

Declutter your computer desktop. Get rid of quick-launch icons and hotlinked programs.

Download a website blocking tool like Stay Focused, Cold Turkey, Nanny, or Aobo. Try one out and see what works for you. Most of these are free, by the way!

Procrastination Note

For those readers who are interested in understanding the pervasive nature of all the social media we are hooked by, I suggest *Irresistible: The Rise of Addictive Technology and the Business of Keeping Us Hooked*, by Adam Alter (2018). It is a powerful and scary book because procrastinators often fall prey to such addictions, which have been designed specifically for our habit.

9. Procrastination Is *Not* a Moral Problem

Too many procrastinators feel guilty about their habit, criticize themselves for giving in to it, and generally beat themselves up way too much. They self-talk and call themselves lazy, stupid, and other negative notions. Procrastination has nothing to do with your goodness, so quit wishing that you were "a better person." Besides, you are not lazy!

This may be surprising, but here's the thing: lazy people almost never have the anxiety, stress, guilt, and shame that procrastinators suffer from. Think about that. They are just lazy people. They feel no shame or guilt; laziness is just who they are. You are a procrastinator with a tough habit—but it's manageable, if you work at it.

Procrastination is not a sign of bad character or weak morality. Never, ever forget this. It's something we have to learn to manage over time. Quit beating yourself up about your procrastination, because it only feeds the cycle of frustration, shame, and guilt.

Some of the finest people I know procrastinate a lot. It has nothing to do with their character or integrity or value. Just have the courage to begin to manage your habit, and get rid of the negative self-judgment.

10. Get an Accountability Partner

This is one of the more intense strategies for dealing with the procrastination habit. It's often used with time management techniques, but it can work with procrastination habits as well.

Put simply, you need to find a friend or colleague whom you respect a lot, who cares about you as a person, and who can be very honest with you. If you pick just any friend, it won't work. You are going to give your word to this person, so who this person is is vitally important. You don't want to disappoint them. You don't want to commit to something and then tell them you didn't do what you said you were going to do.

Having chosen this partner, you simply make a contract with them. Examples of such contracts are "I will complete the first chapter of my dissertation in two months" or "I will make the case to my boss for a raise" or "I will go to Weight Watchers for four weeks." You get the idea. Make a promise that will work toward the elimination of your procrastination habit, and make that promise to someone you respect a great deal. There is a good chance that you will keep your word and complete the task. Giving your word creates a high level of risk, so don't take this suggestion lightly. It's a powerful one to try, and it usually works.

11. Two Ways to Measure Progress: Process and Output

It's very important to have a way to measure your accomplishments so that you have a feedback loop to inform your thinking and your work. There are two basic ways to do this.

- Measure the process of your work, which usually means the amount of time you invest in the task—say, six hours of research for understanding a topic better. You use six hours as your scorecard, divided into 30 minute or one-hour increments that you *visually* record (e.g., checklist, scratch off).

- Measure the output or product you produce. This could be the number of pages you write per day; the number of rooms you clean per shift, the amount of firewood you chop per hour, and so on.

Sometimes you can use both of these methods to measure progress. Ernest Hemingway, the great writer, had both a process and output way to measure his writing production. He almost always wrote standing up, and preferred the early morning hours. He tracked his daily output on a chart. His goals were to write five pages a day or work for five hours, whichever came first.

Stephen King, the prolific thriller writer, tries to write six pages a day. He has written more than 50 novels and sold more than 350 million copies of his work. He almost always accomplishes his daily task of six pages, which really add up quickly. He also sticks to the same routine every day. He has a cup of tea or glass of water and sits down to write around 8:30 in the morning. He sits in the same seat, and all his papers are arranged in the same place. This specific routine sets him up psychologically to start to dream and write.

I do a fair amount of writing in a year and I mark the time allotted—usually five hours a day in 30-minute increments—as the way I measure progress. I used to count the number of pages written, but it didn't work for me. If I was having a difficult day and not producing the number I wanted, I would get frustrated and begin to procrastinate. Use the way that works for you and visually record your progress.

12. Implementation Intentions

Implementation intentions are if-then plans that spell out in advance how you want to strive toward a set goal. Implementation intentions were first introduced by Peter Gollwitzer, a psychologist, back in the 1990s and are known to enhance the rate of goal attainment.

Gollwitzer conducted a research study for people who wanted to exercise. There were two groups. Group A was told to plan when and where they would exercise each week. For example, "I will go to the gym every other day at five o'clock," or "I will go to the gym every day at lunchtime." Group B was given no instructions and didn't plan ahead. The results were that Group B participants only exercised regularly about 30% of the time. Group A participants exercised 91% of the time.

Implementation intentions are a planned response to ensure that goal intentions—which have to be strong—will reflexively lead to the desired behaviors and subsequent attainment of the goal. The basic formula is that if situation X is encountered (an activity, a time, an emotional thought), then I will do Y (the behavior).

Here are some examples:

- *If* I start to feel angry, *then* I will take four deep breaths to calm down.

- *If* I am cashing my paycheck at my bank, *then* I will deposit 5% of it into my savings account.

- *When* I wake up in the morning, I *will* meditate for 10 minutes before doing anything else.

- *When* I get home from work, I *will* check my blood pressure with a monitor.

- *If* it is Sunday, I *will* clean the house for one hour after breakfast.

- *If* I have completed my exercise regimen, then I *will* have a glass of wine with my dinner.

You can use implementation intentions to start something, avoid bad habits, or take advantage of an opportunity. What makes them work is the specificity involved. It's most effective when you note the time, the location, and the specific behavior that will occur.

13. Create an "Unschedule"

This is a counterintuitive strategy created by the psychologist Neil Fiore (2007), which he explains in his excellent book, *The Now Habit*. I think it is most useful for people who have a fair amount of autonomy in the work they do—consultants, the self-employed, freelancers, and gig economy workers. I do think it would be challenging for someone with a regular 9–5 job. Fiore might disagree with my perspective.

I have used some of his thinking to help me become more organized about the right things and build more fun into my life. He has informed my thinking about how I spend most of my weekends, in a mixture of work and play.

I like Fiore's approach to procrastination because it is more humane and holistic than the approaches of many other psychologists. They often use terms like *failure, self-inflicted wound*, and *maladaptive work style* to describe procrastination. I don't find those terms helpful but do find them very judgmental. Given that procrastinators are often self-critical and way too harsh on themselves, they might find Fiore's different approach refreshing.

Fiore believes that procrastinators often think they have 24 hours a day to do what needs to be done. But, after sleep, exercise, family obligations, and personal stuff, there isn't all that much time left. We wonder where all our time went and often feel guilty for not getting more done.

Fiore believes there are a lot of things, times, and responsibilities that are already allocated. We need to highlight these to get an accurate picture of how much time we actually have, to do important work.

This is a brief description of his process:

- Take your weekly/monthly calendar and fill in all the times when you want to have fun. This might be goofing off with family and friends on Saturdays, pizza nights on Tuesdays, or date night with your partner on Fridays.

- Then fill out your obligations *other than* work—for example, your daily exercise time or biweekly attendance at religious services.

- You now have a realistic picture of how much time is actually left to do your professional work. From here, you can create your *unschedule.*

This way you will have a more balanced approach to life and feel less overwhelmed—a kind of stress that procrastinators often feel. This guilt-free plan helps us do the hard work to accomplish our professional responsibilities.

He shares some other interesting ideas. The key to the success of the unschedule is interspersing play with work and achieving more balance. He believes if we work less, we will be more productive.

Many procrastinators resent all the work they "have to do." The unschedule reverses this dynamic dramatically.

Procrastinators often see play as a weakness. Fiore doesn't believe in all play and no work. He understands the importance of doing quality work and that we need uninterrupted time to do "deep work," as Cal Newport describes in his excellent books.

Fiore appreciates enjoying rewards after doing quality work. He suggests 30-minute blocks of focused work with short breaks in between. This is how I organize my own professional work.

As you can see, Fiore's unschedule is a counterintuitive way of dealing with procrastination. Build yourself a realistic picture of the givens in your life, including fun, and *then* address your work time, not the other way around Try it, you might like it.

14. Goal-Setting for Procrastinators

A lot of procrastinators aren't very good at setting goals for two primary reasons: they usually create a gargantuan goal that is unrealistic and then get overwhelmed by the enormity of the tasks involved; *or* they are way too vague about their goals and don't know how or where to begin.

When I talk about goal setting, I mean establishing important personal and professional targets, whether it's getting married or joining the US Navy. Whatever the goal is, it has to matter a lot to you.

There are a few things you need to think about regarding goals.

- The why has to matter and be worthy of your time, attention, and commitment.

- You need a timetable with *specific* time frames like "by the end of the month" or "tomorrow."

- You need a way to measure success. Target "lose eight pounds," *not* "lose some weight." Specificity matters because it provides actionable targets to strive for.

- Have a reward system in place *before* you start the tasks to reach the goal. We know that rewards work, so think about some positive rewards you can earn as you make progress toward your goal, such as a long weekend away with your partners or a dinner with good friends.

- Please write down your goals. The research indicates that this helps with achievement (Karia, 2015; Allen, 2015). Strangely, most people don't write down their goals. Those who do tend to accomplish them. It's a very simple act that reaps great results.

Some Advice

Get a thought partner to help you with your goal setting. A thought partner has to be someone you trust, who knows you well, and who can be very honest with you. Their role is to challenge your thinking so that you don't set yourself up for failure by creating unreachable goals. They are your reality check. They can help you think through some big steps, identify positive rewards, and establish ways to measure success. I use thought partners all the time and so strongly recommend using one.

Expect setbacks because they are out there waiting for you, even if you plan carefully for them. Seneca, the great Roman Stoic philosopher, statesman, and dramatist, shared much wisdom during his life. One of his quotations, which I have in my office, is "Mistakes weigh heavily on those who expect nothing but good fortune." Bad things often happen, so be ready for them psychologically. Think through a plan B from the very beginning, because it will give you confidence.

With big, important goals, it is helpful to conduct a "pre mortem" (Klein, 2007). For a pre mortem, you anticipate what could go wrong with the achievement of your goal *before* you start working on it. This is where a thought partner can come in real handy because it is difficult (though not impossible) to conduct a robust pre mortem by yourself. A partner can capture your thoughts on a flip chart or whiteboard so that they are large enough to see.

A pre mortem is quite counterintuitive because people like to focus on accomplishments, making progress, and being successful, not identifying what could go wrong. But this is a powerful strategy for identifying the potential mud pies that are out there waiting for you to step in them.

A pre mortem works like this: imagine that you are looking back one year from now. Although you worked really hard and put a lot of time in toward your goal, you were unsuccessful in reaching it. Why?

Here's an example. I wanted to finish writing a book about planning implementation tools, but I didn't complete the goal. I sketched out the reasons why not.

- I got lost doing a whole lot of research about implementation and spent too much time reading everything I could about the topic.

- I didn't establish a realistic writing schedule. I tried to write four nights a week, but given my family obligations, I could only carve out two.

- I tried to write *and* edit my work at the same time, so it took forever to complete a chapter.

You get the idea here. Thinking through what could go wrong helps you establish a game plan for moving forward on your goal. You take the reasons why you might not be successful and identify what you will do differently going forward. In my case:

- I will limit my research to 10 hours per week. I already know a great deal about the subject, so I don't need to go overboard in conducting extensive research.

- I need to establish a realistic writing schedule and commit to two nights a week that I dedicate to writing. I also need to find a writing space where I don't have constant interruptions.

- I will write a chapter and call it a *rough* draft before I edit my work. Better yet, I will find a freelance editor to edit my work and save me a lot of time.

That's it in a nutshell. You anticipate what might go wrong. With those issues in mind, you create a realistic game plan going forward. *Don't* forget to incorporate a reward system along the way!

Another example is losing weight. There are billions of dollars spent each year on losing weight. It's a national obsession and a health crisis wrapped together. Using the pre mortem technique can give a person a realistic game plan for losing weight.

Again, you would do this with a thought partner to help you right-size your thinking. Imagine that we are back here six months from now. Although you really tried hard to lose your target of 25 pounds, you barely lost five pounds. Looking back, what went wrong?

- I set myself up for failure at the very beginning by not being realistic about how much weight I could actually lose. Twenty-five pounds was way too much to accomplish.

- I didn't follow through with a disciplined exercise program of walking every day for one hour. When the weather was nice, I did well, but when it rained or was cold, I postponed my exercise regimen.

- I really like some wine with my dinner every night. Sometimes, when I dined out, I treated myself to an extra glass of wine. Those empty calories neutralized my walking calories.

- I usually have a meal bar for breakfast, but I found that I got really hungry around ten thirty or so. When that happened, I had a candy bar to hold me over till lunch.

That's enough mud pies identified. Here's how you would turn them into a game plan with your thought partner.

- I need to be realistic and set a goal of 10-pound weight loss instead of 25 pounds. It took me a lot of time to gain the weight, so I need to be patient about how much time it will take to lose it.

- I realize that when the weather is bad, I procrastinate about my walking hour. I need to join the local YMCA, which is reasonably inexpensive, and walk on their indoor running track when the weather is bad.

- I need to limit my drinking to one glass of wine each night whether I am at home or at a restaurant. Note that I don't say no wine at meals, because that would be unrealistic and feel like deprivation—which procrastinators hate!

The pre mortem is worth a try when setting your goals because it helps identify what could possibly go wrong and helps create realistic strategies to neutralize those challenges.

Procrastination Note

Professor Piers Steel, author of the book *The Procrastination Equation*, has a website procrastinatus.com where you can take a survey on goal attainment. I took it and liked it; it's worth a look. It will show you your level of commitment to accomplish a specific, stated goal. It's very revealing and helpful.

Some Final Words on Goals

There is a helpful book about setting goals by the author Jon Acuff (2017), *Finish: Give Yourself the Gift of Getting Done*, which gives some strong advice about setting most goals: (a) we are almost always too ambitious about what we can actually accomplish, (b) most of the time we should *double* the timeline for an anticipated project, and (c) we should cut our goals in half.

Just think about this. If we follow his advice, I believe we can accomplish more and not feel overwhelmed most of the time.

He also says, "Make it fun, if you want to get done." I think this is wonderful advice and a strong recommendation for the concept of *temptation bundling*. Combine things that you like with the onerous task that you might avoid. Appealing things might include making it a group assignment, playing your favorite music while working, or meeting outside. Reward, reward, reward.

> More than likely, you've spent most of your life choosing to do more than possible and beating yourself up for not being able to keep up.
> —Josh Acuff

There are some goals that you might not be able to cut in half. In that situation, he suggests that you give yourself more time. The bottom line is to learn to take the pressure off because it isn't usually helpful, especially for procrastinators.

Lastly, he shares an interesting concept called *noble obstacles*, which are the things you must finish *before* you can attack your priority goals. Using "until" as an excuse seems respectable on the surface, but can create friction—all the little aggravations and obstacles that get in the way of getting meaningful things done.

For example, say you want to want to clean out your garage. But you come up with the great idea, or noble goal, of having a garage sale *before* tackling the job of actually cleaning out the garage. Sounds great! However, what could have been a straightforward project has just become loaded with details. Picking a date, reviewing homeowners' association rules, making advertising signs, getting tables for display and a host of other details are now part of the task. On the surface, it looks like you are getting all your ducks in row, but it's a form of perfectionism and procrastination. All too often, you get frustrated with these details and quit the project. Sound familiar? Bottom line, set fewer goals and allow for a longer time frame.

A key word to pay attention to is *until*, because it sets up lots of obstacles before you begin . You can't start the project *until* you have done the research, conducted surveys, analyzed the data, created a draft report, sought feedback, and so on. How about starting the writing, seeing what emerges, and worrying about all the *untils* later?

I recently used this approach to start my newest book. My usual practice is to do tons of research before I start to write anything. I mean at least 100 hours of research. This time, I told myself to just start writing about a subject I had a lot of experience with and some knowledge about. I created 60 or more pages in a week. They reflected very rough thinking, but the writing created momentum I have never had before. I gave the pages to a colleague to do some copy editing. She turned the rough draft into a pretty good paper and reduced it to about 40 pages.

At that point, I had created a mostly stress-free first draft. My next step will be to conduct research that will be focused rather than exploratory, to support my ideas. It's a very different approach for me, one that I am confident will enable me to write a good (not *greatest of all time*) book in a lot less time.

15. Eat the Small Frog First

Mark Twain is credited with the saying, "If you have to eat two frogs, eat the big one first." I have never agreed with this idea because it just didn't make sense to me. It might be a good, effective productivity tip, but I don't think it works for most procrastinators. Here's why.

If we have two frogs (difficult, complex, noxious tasks) to eat, our procrastination radar will be in full bloom. There is a very good chance that we will never attempt to eat the big frog first. It will be too uncomfortable. We will get overwhelmed by the distasteful nature of the task and put it on the sideline.

I think procrastinators can use many of the strategies, tools, and techniques in this book to tackle the little frog first. They can make the task more "chewable" by slicing it into smaller parts—an effective approach to a noxious or overwhelming task. They don't have to eat it all at once, but in small parts over time. They can bundle it with something pleasant—say some ketchup or mustard—to make it more palatable.

Build in rewards along the way. Don't wait until the very end of the process. Remember, rewards are powerful things. They can create a scorecard that marks progress (e.g., how much of the frog has been eaten).

Having eaten the small frog, the procrastinator will have a set of practices and strategies to apply to eating the big frog. They can apply what they have learned in completing the smaller, less risky task to successfully tackling the bigger one.

I think many people have taken Twain's misdirected quote and made it very difficult to tackle big, uncomfortable tasks. Consider tackling the smaller task first and see what happens.

16. Temptation Bundling

This idea comes from Professor Katherine Milkman of the Wharton School of Business. She found that she had real difficulty going to the gym and exercising every day. So she used a guilty pleasure to motivate herself to go to the gym. She listened to her favorite audiobooks as she exercised, and her gym attendance improved dramatically.

I use this technique when invoicing clients for consulting work. I am very bad with details (e.g., mileage, flights, parking fees, meals) and avoid them if I can. But I also need to get paid. So I do my invoicing while watching a sporting event on TV. It takes two or three times as long to create an accurate invoice, but it doesn't matter to me, because the task actually gets done and I enjoy sports a lot.

Other examples of temptation bundling could be doing housework while listening to your favorite music, or treating yourself to a latte while reading a long research report. The key is to make the onerous chore more attractive *in any way you can.* Don't get caught up in self-sabotaging thinking that says, *I shouldn't need something nice to help me with an onerous task.* If bundling works, use it and ignore the silly self-talk.

A Powerful Story about Temptation Bundling

Dan Ariely is an American-Israeli professor and author who has written several intriguing and informative books. He has a fascinating story to share that provides some insight into the power of temptation bundling.

As a young man, he contracted hepatitis C from a blood transfusion and was given the powerful drug Interferon to combat the disease. He had to inject himself three times a week with the drug, which had severe side effects. He would get intense chills and vomit a great deal. In short, he was in a very tough situation that would have been easy to skip or avoid entirely.

This is what Ariely did. He simply loved movies and would go to the video store on the mornings of his injections. He picked out several really interesting movies. He carried them in his backpack all day, anticipating the pleasure he would get by viewing them. In the late afternoon, he would inject himself with the Interferon and start his movies. In about an hour, the chills and vomiting would begin. He toughed them out until they subsided, all the while watching movies. His doctors told him that he was the only patient they knew who had consistently injected himself and cured the disease.

Ariely had created a strong connection between something he loved and something noxious and uncomfortable. He created a powerful habit that was reinforced by a reward. Think about using this technique when you have to do something you really don't like but still needs to be done. Combine the task with something really enjoyable.

Procrastination Research Note

Professor Kathleen Milkman, whom I mentioned earlier, conducted a study with 226 students and faculty who were having trouble going to the gym and exercising. She separated the participants into three groups:

- Group 1 got an iPad loaded with cool audiobooks, which they could only access at the gym.

- Group 2 had the audiobooks added to their own iPads, and were encouraged to listen to them only at the gym.

- Group 3 got a gift certificate and were encouraged to work out more.

The results: Group 1 worked out 29% more than Group 2 and 59% more than Group 3. So bundling works. Try it!

17. If You Are Working with a Peer Who Procrastinates, Some Advice

If you have a procrastinating colleague, it can be a challenge to work with them, especially if your work is dependent on them getting their things done. One of the most important things a procrastinator needs to understand is that their inconsistency can create distrust among colleagues and team members. This has nothing to do with honesty or integrity; it's the consequence of their procrastination habit.

It's important to address the issue of a procrastinating colleague with care and clarity. Being nice yet vague doesn't help; neither does being aggressive and explicit. Here are some things to consider.

It's important to assume that procrastinators are well-intentioned people who procrastinate. There isn't some nefarious motivation. Understanding this will enable you to deal with them with empathy.

Be as direct as you can. Here are some things that can work to address specific issues.

- Procrastinators are pretty bad at estimating how much time and effort something will take. You can offer to be a thought partner and help them create reasonable deadlines and workloads. Ask questions like "When you have done something like this in the past, how long did it take?" or "What obstacles do you anticipate with this assignment?" If they don't identify any, then you need to do that for them if you can, because the obstacles are there.

- You can also help the procrastinator create a realistic visual picture of the available time to complete the task, and identify milestones along the way. Figure out an achievable deadline. Work backwards to create a series of milestones toward completing the project. This way you can help the procrastinator track progress and avoid the crushing stress of rushing to get done at the last minute.

- You can also act as an accountability partner. Make an agreement on a deadline and a strong consequence for not fulfilling their commitment to that deadline (e.g. a cash payment, time contributed to a chore for you). Be there to help them, but don't let them slide or make excuses.

18. The Powerful Myth of Multitasking

This is not a specific strategy but rather a pitfall that every procrastinator needs to be aware of. Almost everyone engages in multitasking during their day. It can feel busy and productive because we seem to be doing so much, but in reality, we are doing very little.

There is an informative book, *The Distracted Mind* (2016), by Adam Gazzaley and Larry D. Rosen, which states that multitasking causes safety risks. A powerful example they cite is that smartphone use while driving a car dramatically increases the risk of a crash. They assert that inattention due to smartphone use causes 23% of all US crashes!

A study at the University of London found that participants who multitask during cognitive tasks experienced IQ score declines that were similar to what they would expect if they had smoked marijuana or stayed up all night. IQ drops among multitasking men lowered their scores to the average range of an eight-year-old.

Dscout.com is a research platform that conducted an amazing study. Its researchers found that we touch our smartphones an average of 2,617 time a day—and this was in 2017! Think about that for a minute. We are tapping, swiping, and clicking all over the place. This destroys concentration and attention. For procrastinators, this is an alarming statistic. We are prone to distractions, and we have information at our fingertips anytime we want to avoid a task. There are thousands of research studies that align with this information.

Just putting your smartphone in another room could be powerful practice that would enable you to focus on what matters. This will not be easy to do. A lot of people, not just procrastinators, have a mild addiction to smartphones. *Entrepreneur* magazine reported a research study that found that 68% of all adults have an irrational fear of losing their smartphones.

The obvious point here is that our smartphones are wonderful devices and at the same time powerful distraction machines. Consider limiting use of your smartphone for a while and see if your procrastination diminishes. At least once a day, I put my smartphone in another room and turn the ringer off. Initially I found that, if the phone was just in another room, when I could hear a faint ring, it drew my attention. Turning the sound off is crucial. I did this for an hour at a time to start, and now I can tolerate several hours at a time without the ever-present phone.

19. Use Visualization to See Yourself Accomplishing Your Goals

There are hundreds of books and articles about the power and effectiveness of visualization. Many world-class athletes use visualization as a daily practice to picture their success. Procrastinators can benefit from this practice by using it to picture the successful completion of a goal or task.

The good news is, like meditation skills, it's easy to develop visualization skills. The key is to create a great deal of *specificity*. For example, say I want to visualize a productive and fulfilling day. I wouldn't just visualize myself working hard and being happy at the end of the day. I would paint a detailed picture of my upcoming day.

- Get up at 6:00 a.m.

- Drink a glass of water.

- Do 10 minutes of stretching exercises.

- Take a long shower.

- Eat a healthy breakfast of scrambled eggs and yogurt, and drink a cup of good coffee that smells great.

- Start my project and work for 30 minutes.

- Take a 10-minute break *with no social media.*

- Continue in a sequence of 30-minute work slots with 10-minute breaks until 12:30 p.m.

- Eat Caesar salmon for lunch and go for a 30-minute walk, for a total lunch break of one hour.

- Check emails for 20 minutes and respond only to the important ones.

- Make phone calls for 30 minutes.

- Take a break (social media OK this time) for 15 minutes.

- Wrap up the final hour with some great music.

- Use that hour to organize for the next day.

- Do some light reading.

- Meditate for 10 minutes.

- Journal about what I accomplished and how I feel about the day.

- Have a nice dinner with family/friends.

- Go to bed at10:00 p.m.

I could easily double the level of detail with this visualization exercise, but you get the idea. Picture a great workday in detail with some variety and success. Note where are you working, what clothes you are wearing, and what music you are playing. Fill in the picture as much as you can, so it becomes a mental map of your day. This way you are being conscious and clear about what you want to accomplish and how you want to conduct your day.

20. Only Focus on the Next Action Step

Procrastinators can get overwhelmed quickly, causing their habit to kick in big-time. We tend to look at the whole mess and not know where to begin. A lot of the writers and researchers who understand this dynamic have one strong suggestion: focus *only* on the next action you can take.

Any project takes real time and attention and has many steps. Create an action plan of those steps, and then focus *only* on the very next step. after you have created a work/action plan. For example, let's say you're writing a paper.

1. Pick the topic for the paper.

2. Give it a title, which helps create focus.

3. Do some research on the topic, but limit it to a specific time frame.

4. Create a draft outline to help organize your thinking.

5. Create a very rough draft of the paper—you aren't looking for top quality yet.

6. Edit the draft or have someone else edit it.

7. Review the edited draft once, and revise to enhance it if you can.

Once again, I could double this list of steps, but these are the large, essential steps necessary to write a paper. The key things to remember are to take it one step at a time and reward yourself after each completed step, not just at the end.

A thought partner can be helpful to create a realistic time allotment for each step, particularly the research step. You can also use your past experience to see how long similar papers have taken.

Remember, conducting extensive research might not be a good use of your time. The goal is to *write* the paper, not do endless research, which can be a form of procrastination. My dissertation chair told me, "Sanaghan, you get paid to write, not read," because he knew I enjoyed the research part a lot more than the writing part.

Whatever the task, break it down into chewable chunks. If your house needs painting, paint one side of the house per day—or just paint the shutters first. Focusing on the next action—painting the window frame—can make the task less daunting and move you forward. Sounds simple, but it isn't. The very next action is the key to success, not biting off the whole thing.

21. Reduce the Number of Decisions You Have to Make

There is a thing called "decision fatigue" (Baumeister & Tierney, 2011), which is a deterioration of the quality of decisions you make over time.

This has big implications for procrastinators. We tend to delay making decisions, especially hard ones. You want as much good decision-making capacity as you can get.

Always try to do you goal-setting or agenda-setting at the *end* of each day. That way, when you start to work the next day, you don't have to decide what you are going to do. The game plan is already there for you. This is a time management technique that I have used, and it works for me. I almost always have my agenda for the day written the night before. It creates a good beginning and positive momentum. Obviously it can change, but I at least have a road map.

It's a challenge to set this habit because we are usually a little tired at the end of the day. But it's a great habit to develop. You set yourself up for success and reduce the friction of starting. Make sure that you reward yourself after you write your to-do list or agenda.

Some famous people, including Barack Obama, Steve Jobs, and Mark Zuckerberg, limit their clothing selections to a minimum, like Steve Jobs's black sweaters and jeans. These individuals don't have to decide what to wear every day. Keep it simple.

There is a fair amount of research showing that having too many choices can get in the way of making good decisions. Sounds counterintuitive, but it's true. For procrastinators, who often like lots of choices (Steel, 2013), this is a real problem. As we search for ever more options, we delay making a decision.

Try to reduce the number of decisions you need to make by making them ahead of time. Set out your gear the night before. Schedule you weekly exercise. Create a to-do list and stick to it. Do whatever you can to avoid decision fatigue and make better decisions.

Procrastination Note

There are two excellent books about decision-making that are counter-intuitive and deeply informative. Barry Schwartz (2004), a psychologist, has written a book, *The Paradox of Choice: Why Less is More*. (He's also given a great TED Talk by that title. Sheena Iyenga (2010), who also gave a TED Talk, wrote the book *The Art of Choosing*.

A brief summary for procrastinators and others to consider is this. The more choices we have, the less likely we are to make good decisions. More is not better. Too many choices can create anxiety and stress (sound familiar?). There is ample evidence that having 3–5 choices is more than good enough, and three choices are probably best.

This resonates with me a great deal. For years I created a whole lot of choices for important decisions, because I thought this was a smart thing to do. I mistakenly thought that more was better, and I got bogged down exploring all the possibilities. It wasn't very smart or effective.

Chapter 4

38 Simple, Practical Tips, Hacks, Tools, and Techniques to Help with Procrastination

Putting things off is the biggest waste of life: it snatches away each day as it comes, and denies us the present by promising the future. The greatest obstacle to living is expectancy, which hangs upon tomorrow and loses today … The whole future lies in uncertainty: live immediately.

—Seneca

1. The Five-Minute Technique

This notion has been around for years. Many authors say it can create positive momentum and a feeling of accomplishment. David Allen, who has written many great books about time management and productivity, is credited with this suggestion. Set a timer for five minutes and start a task. After five minutes have gone by, signaled by the timer, check in with yourself and see how you are feeling and thinking. Often, *not always*, people will continue the task for another five minutes or more.

Remember, getting started is one of the most difficult parts of the procrastination habit. Try a task for five minutes and see what happens. What's five minutes?

2. Watch Your Commitments

Lots of procrastinators have a difficult time saying no. They take on way too many requests to help others. They tend to overcommit and set themselves up for failure. Above all, they *avoid their own work*.

You need to be selective about what you say yes to, because others will fill up your schedule if you let them. There is an excellent book, *The Power of a Positive No*, by William Ury (2007), which is a great resource for anyone who has a hard time saying no. It's especially helpful for procrastinators. And in chapter 6, I will share some effective ways to say no to people and not offend them.

A final note about this hack: lazy people are very good at enrolling others to help them do their work. They also know that most people are "nice" and want to be helpful, making others soft touches for them. Almost always, when a lazy person asks for help, you are being manipulated. Be conscious of this and learn to say no, strongly and politely.

3. Lower your standards

Procrastinators (as well as many other people) often have very high expectations and standards for themselves and tend to overreach. Instead of trying to write 20 pages a day, strive for 10. Instead of attempting 30 minutes of meditation, try 10. Instead of trying to do 50 push-ups, try for 10. Ten isn't a magical number, but it is a *realistic* number.

Accomplish the 10s and see what happens. If you can do more, great, but don't set yourself up for failure from the very beginning. "Start small to go big" is a mantra you should have on your workstation wall. It's an important principle for procrastinators to understand.

4. Announce Your Intention(s) to Others

This is similar to have an accountability partner, because you put your word on the line by declaring an intention. Communicating to others what you intend to do can be just enough pressure to get you moving toward your goal. You don't want to disappoint coworkers, friends, or family.

Try it at first with a *moderately* risky task, not something big and bold and high stakes. Pick something doable yet important, and let people know what you want to accomplish, accompanied by a deadline. Some people use Facebook or other social media to make these commitments.

5. The Why You Are Doing Something Can Be Helpful

Remembering the purpose you are trying to achieve can be highly motivating. For example, if you are procrastinating on writing a paper for a college course, think about how this task will get you closer to achieving your degree. This in turn will enable you to get a better job and provide for your family, or make a contribution to your organization by doing relevant research.

The why matters, so think about it. Post it somewhere highly visible so you can revisit it often. This is a technique I have used and found helpful. Some of my colleagues have pictures of their dream (e.g., vacation house, trip to Africa, graduation photo) in full view so that they can see what they are trying to achieve on a daily basis.

6. Shut Your Door

Lots of procrastinators are highly distractible (Steel, 2007; Pychyl, 2013), so you need to minimize your distractions. If you have an open door, people can pop in throughout the day to say hello or complain. You also might get distracted by watching who passes by and wondering what they are doing. Shut your door periodically so you can focus on the task at hand. Some people have their desks facing away from their doors. That sounds simple, but it also works.

In COVID-19 times, many of us have blurred boundaries between home and work. The distractions are all over the place. You have to find a way to be by yourself whenever possible. I realize that this is a challenge for many people, but be creative in finding a quiet place to do your most important work.

I have friends who swap their kids every other day, sharing child-watching responsibilities. One day all the kids are at one home; the second day they go to the other home. The children love the variety, and it creates a consistently quiet workplace for the collaborating parents during the week.

7. Think about David Allen's Two-Minute Rule

Allen (2015), the time management and productivity guru, tells us that if you can do a task in two minutes, just go ahead and do it. Simple and quick things like feeding the cat, taking out the garbage, or putting away the dishes don't take much time or thought, so just do the thing and get it out of the way as quickly as you can. It helps to clear your mind of the distraction caused by all the little things you have to do.

8. Take Short Breaks

Taking breaks helps with concentration, production, and momentum, so use them throughout the day. The well-known Pomodoro technique is an example. Use a timer and work for 25 minutes. Then take a five-minute break. You might not be able to do 25 minutes of work initially, and that's fine. Work your way up to the 25-minute allotment.

Don't try to slog straight through several hours of research, cleaning, or other challenging work. Take short 5–10 minute breaks throughout the day. It works.

Try mightily *not* to surf social media during your breaks. You could get lost in space and spend way too long reading stuff that doesn't matter.

I have found that I can concentrate for about 30 minutes when I am researching or writing. I take a 10-minute break every half hour. I find it helps sustain my energy and interest. Whenever I push to do more than 30 minutes at a time, I tend to wander and get distracted. You have to find the time frame that works for you. Don't set yourself up for failure by being too ambitious with your expectations

10. Write Things Down

Procrastinators, like other people, have ideas, thoughts, and worries buzzing around in their heads. This can be both distracting and anxiety-producing. Commit to writing down what you need to accomplish. It will quiet the buzzing and help you focus on what needs to be done.

I have a small notepad on my desk. When an idea or something I need to remember pops into my head, I write it down right away. It helps me get back to what I need to be doing. Later I look at the list and see if I need to move on something, make a decision, or call someone.

Have some kind of idea-catching system, because ideas come out all the time. Creativity experts tell us to make sure we use a journal or an app like Evernote to capture our notions, because often creative idea are fleeting. We tell ourselves that we will remember them, but we don't.

So writing things down is a twofer: you clear your head of distracting ideas, and you capture the best for review later.

11. Build a Small Ritual to Get Started

The strategy of creating rituals has been around a long time and can be a powerful mechanism to get things moving. For example, when I go walking, I always put on my hat first and then my shoes. I *always* store them in the same place. The hat signals to me that I intend to go walking. I do 10,000 steps a day consistently, rain or shine, and have had this little hat ritual for many years. It yields about a 95% success rate.

Many world-class athletes have specific rituals that help them work out for several hours at a time. Often conditioning is tedious work, but it needs to be done if they are to maintain peak physical fitness. They go through the same routine every day. A routine facilitates action because it is predictable, has chewable chunks, and provides some variety.

For others, having a pad of paper and a pen on their desk helps them focus on the first task of the day. Still others get a cup of coffee first thing, chat with colleagues for 10 minutes, and then sit down to work. Create your own personal ritual that will get you moving and acting.

There are a couple of books I recommend reading about creating rituals and habits. One is *Atomic Habits* by James Clear (2019). The other is *Mini Habits: Smaller Habits, Bigger Results*, by Stephen Guise (2013).

12. Try to Be Realistic

Most of us have a strong tendency to either overestimate or underestimate how long a task will take or how hard it will be to complete (Steel, 2007; Pychyl, 2013; Salzberger, 2017). For those who tend to underestimate, build in some extra time to complete the task. I have this tendency and have learned to add at least 20% more time to important tasks, as a general rule. It seems to be helpful most of the time.

If you overestimate, get a reality check from a friend or coworker. Overestimation can kick the procrastination habit into high gear. Your self-talk goes like this: *This will take 10 hours at least, and I only have a couple hours available. I will wait until I have the 10 hours next week to tackle this assignment.* You get the picture. We make it daunting from the very beginning. So get a reality check if you can.

I often ask someone who has done a similar task how long and hard it was. I almost always get great advice and often lower my estimation. The key here is to be realistic, because both under- and overestimation can trigger the procrastination habit.

13. Build Small Habits

S. J. Scott (2017) is a habit-building expert. His book *Habit Stacking* has over a hundred ideas for building habits. One of his best pieces of advice is this: *"The easiest way to build a new habit is to **start really small"**.* This is an important thing to remember. Don't try to change a negative habit overnight or implement a new practice immediately. If you're trying to build an exercise habit, consider going to the gym twice this week and three times next week. Build your attendance over time. Remember, smaller can be better than trying for a home run and striking out!

Starting small is a theme throughout this book because it has a powerful effect on procrastinators, who are often overly optimistic about what they can accomplish. It's a counterintuitive notion for many people, who have been taught to go big or go home. I see that as a mean and silly aspiration. If you can train yourself to actually do something meaningful and small, then over time you will build your capacity to do larger, more complex tasks and feel successful.

14. Use a Distraction Log

For a couple of days, write down everything that distracts you. This is an adaptation of a the more common time log, in which you write down what you are doing in 15-minute increments for a week to see how you actually use your time. I found that a lot of people get tired of the time log after the second or third day and simply don't complete it. The distraction log is much easier to implement and can be just as informative.

For a week, try to capture each time you are distracted or interrupted by others. Distractions might be an unexpected visit from a colleague, a student dropping in outside of office hour, a call to attend an unexpected meeting, loud noises, or emails dinging away. If you can log distractions for at least three days, you will see how often you get drawn away from your work.

Then the hard work comes into play: you have to create plans to eliminate some of the distractions and interruptions. For example, you might have a daily meeting *by yourself* for an hour. Close your office door or go someplace else for the quiet, distraction-free meeting by yourself.

You might find that one or two colleagues are always dropping in during office hours to chat, problem solve, or gossip. Once you know who they are, meet with them and agree on a scheduled time to talk, preferably over lunch or a morning cup of coffee.

One of the hidden dynamics of interruptions is that many people like them. They can make you feel important because people are seeking you out for advice, conversation, or gossip. Managing distractions can create the space and time to get things done and eliminate switching costs associated with interruptions.

15. Surround Yourself with Non-Procrastinators

If you tend to procrastinate, try to work on a team whose other members *don't* procrastinate. The peer pressure created about getting things done will help motivate you to be in service to the team and not disappoint them.

I used this protocol early in my career for my first book. I joined a group of experienced writers who met every two weeks. Attendance was close to 100% every week for over a year. It really helped me commit to doing the writing I needed to do, because I didn't want to disappoint them or break my word. I also appreciated that they were experiencing many of the same challenges I was in writing a book. It helped me feel less strange and not alone with my struggles.

People who want to make running a daily practice often join a running club. I have a colleague who has run almost every day with the same group of runners for six years. She loves the camaraderie of the group and wouldn't dream of not showing up because she didn't *feel* like it.

16. What Would a Really Smart or Wise Person Do?

Sometimes we get caught up in overanalyzing—making things more complicated than they are or getting stuck about how to move forward. It might be helpful to think of a colleague, friend, or role model who is really smart or wise or both. Ask yourself:

- "What would Mary do here?"

- "How would Rahim approach this problem?"

- "What information would William want in solving this challenge?"

- "What creative approach would Maureen have to this situation?"

Sometimes thinking about your situation from another person's perspective can free up the logjam in your mind and get things moving in the right direction.

17. Make an Accomplishment List

Too often, procrastinators focus on what they don't do and forget or dismiss what they actually do. It's a helpful reminder to write down your accomplishments weekly and place the list in full view so you can reread it and congratulate yourself. It can be a wonderful motivator and provide a more balanced view than just focusing on the disappointments.

This is a technique that I use in my professional life. I do a lot of writing, and I procrastinate on some of it. On my office wall, I have a list of my most recently published papers and books. It's written on bright yellow paper that I can see from across the room. It's a gentle reminder that I have completed a lot of writing. It helps motivate me to work on the articles I am procrastinating about.

People want to feel that they can be successful with a given task, which builds confidence. A visual reminder of what you have already done can help. Think about all the sports teams that have won-lost scorecards displayed prominently in their locker rooms. Keeping score is a smart strategy.

18. Make Transitions Easy

This piece of advice builds on the notion of friction—all those little things that get in our way or distract us. If we encounter a lot of hurdles, the procrastination habit kicks in. If you have to clear your desk or reorganize your filing system *before* you begin to write, you will tend to procrastinate.

Make getting down to work as easy as possible. Instead of clearing your home office (a den of distractions), work at the dining room table with just your computer, a pen, and some paper. Keep it simple.

19. Find Your Best Time to Work

People have their own work rhythms—the times when they work best and feel like they are "in the flow." For me it's between 9:00 a.m. and 2:00 p.m. most days. That's when I feel ready to work. I have made my transitions easy and can be very productive. I am OK until around five o'clock, but the earlier time frame is my sweet spot. I do low-leverage tasks in the late afternoon and save my hard lifting for my morning sweet spot.

One of my colleagues' best time to work is from one to five o'clock most days. She is not a morning person at all. She does nonessential tasks then and holds her sweet spot sacred. She doesn't let people distract her then and minimizes interruptions.

Remember: if you are tired, you will tend to procrastinate (Steel, 2007).

20. Focus on Effort, Not Outcome, When You Reward Yourself

This is a key theme to remember and a choice-point for people. If you write for several hours, reward yourself along the way. Don't focus on outcome, like the number of pages). Focus on the act of progress being made.

Too many of us get caught up in tallying the number of pages written, the number of reports read, or the number of proposals completed. All are good things to accomplish but might take way too long to complete. If you are continuing to work and be productive, focus on rewarding that behavior.

21. "Constructive" Procrastination

When you feel like you are beginning to procrastinate on a task, and if you have tried mindfulness and it's not working, stop the task you are working on and work on something else. This could be a lower-priority task (we usually have scores of these) that you still need to accomplish sometime. Keep a "to-do someday" list for this situation. That way, you will continue doing something productive. Lower-priority tasks are usually easier to do, so your resistance to them might be less intense. At least you will have gotten something done and have a small sense of accomplishment. This will feel good and might motivate you to get back to the original task.

22. Think about Getting a Standing Desk or Desk Converter

Texas A&M (2016) published research in "Boosting Productivity at Work May Be Simple: Stand Up" that found that employees who used standing desks were 46% more productive than those who sat at traditional desks. I have tried using a standing desk several times, and it seems to energize me. Just changing your physical position can provide variety in your work life. If you feel like you are about to procrastinate, use your standing desk or desk converter to change your energy, refocus, and keep working.

A colleague of mine recently used this technique with a project she was stalled on. She bought a desk converter and started to use it. She communicated that it helped create bursts of energy for her as she rotated between standing and sitting on a regular basis.

Use whatever you can to move things forward, whether that is a change of scenery, alternately standing and sitting, or stretching during breaks. Get some energy!

23. The Raymond Chandler Technique

Raymond Chandler was a prolific writer who set aside four hours each day for writing. During this time, he didn't force himself to write, but he also didn't let himself do anything else. He wouldn't read, write a letter, or clean his desk—he did *nothing else.*

This takes some real discipline, but I have used this technique in one-hour time slots and it seems to work well about 50% of the time. This is a pretty good success rate, so consider trying it out.

Notice that I didn't say I did *great* writing during this time slot. The point is that I usually got down to writing something, which is the goal. Remember Chandler's motto: "WRITE OR DO NOTHING AT ALL." I have it posted in my office in plain view.

24. Use Two Devices if You Can

When we do our work on computers, we can be easily derailed because we are always close to immediate distractions. We can check email, browse social media, or play games. One powerful technique is to configure your work computer to be free from all the apps we love, reserving it for work only. Have another device, like an iPad, for distractions like games, shopping, and social media. One device is strictly for work, the other for play.

25. Your Smartphone Is a Time-Wasting Attention Grabber

Research has shown that we check our smartphones hundreds of times a day. In fact, in one study (King Online University), people touched their phones an average of 2,617 times per day! That's ridiculous. That's about a million touches a year!

I love my iPhone, but I am very conscious about how I use it. I track my time on the phone on a weekly basis and try to keep it to a minimum. I realize that this is not feasible for a lot of people, but if you can dramatically reduce your checking, swiping, tapping, and touching, you will be more productive and tend to procrastinate less.

Most of us don't need to be connected all the time, but there is some research that shows that if we don't have access to our phones, we can get anxious and irritable. Some people even show psychological symptoms similar to substance addiction (Alter, 2017). If you want to learn more about the addictive nature of our smartphones, I suggest Alter's book *Irresistible: The Rise of Addictive Technology and the Business of Keeping Us Hooked.* It's a fascinating and scary read and shows how these devices have been designed to be addictive

My other strong suggestion here is to put your phone away somehow—put it in another room (the best solution) or just turn it off completely. Try it for 30 minutes, then an hour. If you can do more than that, great. But one hour smartphone-free will provide you with quality time to do something productive and worthwhile.

One note: there are very few real emergencies in our lives when someone we love is in danger. So folks who use this as an excuse are fooling themselves and are probably great procrastinators.

26. The Seinfeld Strategy

Having a visual cue can trigger you to action. Visual reminders can motivate, inspire, or drive you to complete the task. The famous comedian Jerry Seinfeld writes jokes every day. He uses a big wall calendar and crosses off each day he writes jokes, so he has a visible reminder of his accomplishment. Once you have a chain of crosses, it can be a motivator to continue the chain of success. Your job then becomes "don't break the chain."

I have used an adaptation of this strategy for measuring how many steps I take each day. My goal is 10,000 steps a day. When I accomplish this, I have a large chart in my office on which I write down the number of steps I have taken. In the past six months, I have only missed one day due to sickness. My average number of steps is around 11,000 per day. I love putting down the number on my wall chart and believe the chart has helped me keep the chain alive.

I used to procrastinate about walking because I was so busy, and walking that many steps takes a lot of time (1 hour 20 minutes). But I want to be healthy, so I do it daily and am proud about it. I also tried listening to audiobooks while I walk, as a type of temptation bundling. That didn't work very well for me, so I have learned to read articles while I walk.

27. Take Three Deep Breaths

Deep breathing is a hack a colleague shared with me several years ago. She too is a productive procrastinator and has used this simple technique anytime she feels anxious or overwhelmed. When the feelings start, she takes three slow, deep breaths and pays attention to how she is feeling—*without* any judgments (e.g., *I shouldn't feel this way* or *Why am I feeling this now?).*

Usually, though not always, three deep breaths are enough to calm her down so she can sit through the thoughts and surf the feelings. They tend to lessen in intensity, and she can then focus on her task at hand. Her self-reported success rate is about 50%, which is a great rate. I have tried the technique many times and it works about 30% of the time for me. I think that with practice and some patience, I can up my success rate over time.

28. Have Really, Really Small Daily Goals

This idea comes from Tim Ferris, who is a great and prolific author of many books well worth reading (e.g., *Tools of the Titans, The 4-Hour Work Week*). I mentioned this example earlier: Ferris asked a fellow writer how he was able to write more than 60 books. "What's your secret?"

The writer's reply stunned him. *"Its easy,I try to write 2 "crappy" pages a day."* He didn't say two really good pages; he said two crappy ones. His big secret was to have really small goals every day. Over time, small goals can grow into big accomplishments. It's an important concept for procrastinators to think about.

When we have big tasks, we can get overwhelmed quickly, and the procrastination machine starts to churn. But almost anyone can write two crappy pages a day. Focus on the production, not the quality, because you can improve the quality later.

I do a lot of research and writing every day. If I produce two pages of pretty good stuff per day, in six months I will have close to 300 pages of writing. With editing, this might get pared down to 250 pages, but that's enough for a book. If I write two books a year, I will be a prolific writer. Think about that. How many people do you know who write two books a year, two pages at a time?

Think about how you can utilize this practice in areas other than writing. Maybe doing chores around the house for 10 minutes? Cleaning the garage for 15 minutes? Weeding the garden for 5 minutes? Small really is beautiful. Over time, you can accumulate successes and accomplish big and important things.

29. Use the Mel Robbins Five-Second Technique

Mel Robbins (2017) is a television host and author of several books. He wrote a book called *The 5 Second Rule*. Briefly, the hack goes like this: Robbins believes that we need to push ourselves to do the hard stuff. If you have the instinct or urge to do something meaningful and connected to a goal, and you don't do it within five seconds, your brain will "kill" the instinct to act. She suggests that you start to count backward from five. By the time you reach one, move to action of some kind. For example, if your urge is to write, sit down at your desk. If your urge is to clean, pick up a sponge. If your urge is to exercise, grab your car keys so you can drive to the fitness place.

The crucial point is to move, act, do something physical. I have tried it several times when I need to get up but am tempted to hit the snooze button. It works. I haven't tried it on more complicated tasks, but it's worth a shot. Start counting!

30. Don't Forget the Old "Swiss Cheese" Time Management Hack

Often, procrastinators think that with a big task, you have to start at the beginning. Not so. For example, when writing a book, you can start wherever you want to. In fact many writers do their introductions last.

When I write, I try to create a rough draft of an outline. Then I start wherever I want, usually what interests me the most. I hate the detailed reference section the most, so I always do that last. I use a lot of tools and techniques to get me through that difficult task (e.g., rewards, temptation bundling, lots of breaks, 10-minute work sessions).

When painting a house, which is a very big task, you might want start with the parts of the house where you can stand comfortably on the ground and paint something within reach. The common wisdom is that you should start at the top of the house and work your way down. Not true. Back in the day, I painted houses all summer at the Jersey Shore to pay for college. We had a crew of five or six guys, and we always started painting at the ground level. It surprised our customers, but it was the easiest way to start—no ladders needed—and about half the house got painted very quickly. We also let the painters paint the sections they liked or were good at.

The point of these techniques is to poke holes in the task and do small parts of it over time. Don't get trapped into thinking you have to start at the beginning. Do what comes easy and gain some momentum.

I mentioned earlier that you can read this book any way you want. There are a lot of different parts to choose from. You don't have to read the whole thing (though I hope you do), just the parts that interest you. You might find that you read more of the book if you find it helpful. But start with an interesting section and see what happens.

31. Consider Shifting Your Thinking

The shift I have in mind is from "I *have* to finish this project" (which can cause resentment and resistance) to "I *choose* to start this project." This notion comes from Neil Fiore (2007), author of *The Now Habit*, one of my favorite books about procrastination. The key theme is not to worry about finishing; focus on starting only.

Ask yourself, "What can I start to do in the next 10 to 15 minutes?" This is specific and tangible, versus the vague notion of "finishing" sometime in the distant future. The notion that you are choosing to start is empowering. Fiore tells us to watch our negative self-talk (*I "should" be doing this*) because it sets us up for failure.

Something to consider when you feel you are starting to procrastinate: try to remove the "shoulds" from your inner dialogue. They are just not helpful.

Procrastination Note

Dr. Albert Ellis was a famous psychologist who developed rational emotive therapy back in the 1950s. He has a pretty powerful idea worth considering: "*If it should be different, it would be. But it's not. This is exactly the way it should be.*" Save yourself from self-criticism and from believing that things should be different. Ellis advises us to choose supportive and comforting phrases, like "I want to," "I get to;" and "I choose to."

32. Massage Yourself

I have a friend who has a lounge chair that has a built-in massage feature. He frequently uses this in between work sessions to give himself a nice reward. It also relaxes him. It's a twofer in terms of benefits. He stays away from social media during his breaks. He might read something interesting while in his special chair, listen to his favorite music, or just sit and enjoy the experience. One last note—he doesn't sit in the chair outside his work hours, because he wants to reserve it only for his work reward.

33. Kindness Matters

Treat yourself like you would treat a close friend. Be kind to yourself. You wouldn't be harsh or critical or judgmental to a close friend about their missteps. You would treat them with respect and care. Do the same for yourself. This is aligned with the notion of self-compassion that I talked about earlier in this book. People tend to be way too harsh on themselves, and it doesn't help. Get rid of the notion that being self-critical and tough on yourself is an "adult" thing to do. It isn't. It's a myth, and it has hurt way too many people for way too long.

When you start to feel some anxiety or dread about a task, use this as a signal to *do something* that will change the feeling quickly (e.g., take a quick walk, take three deep breaths). And quit being unkind to yourself.

34. Run a Dash

This notion comes from a company called 43 Folders, which does a lot of work in the time management and productivity arena. They have an interesting web page, 43Folders.com, which is worth a look. This is a different version of chewable chunks and short bursts of work I have mentioned earlier. I really like the term "dash" because it has some energy behind it.

There are three kinds of dashes:

1. In the time-based dash, you choose a certain amount of time in which to do something that is achievable and not intimidating. The company suggests a time frame of eight minutes, which is just enough to see a little progress and maybe even create momentum.

2. In the unit-based dash, you agree to work through an arbitrary number of pieces associated with your project, such as words

written, pages read, loads of laundry dried, or rooms cleaned.

3. In the combination dash, you get to stop an aggravating task when you reach the time goal or the unit goal—whichever comes first.

The key, in my view, is the eight minutes, which is a bearable time frame for most tasks and enough time to see progress. Try it, because it's not a big investment of time or energy.

35. Use the DUST Model of Procrastination

The DUST model was created by Graham Allcott (2014), founder of Think Productive and the author of *A Practical Guide to Productivity*. This simple and effective model helps you figure out *why* you might be procrastinating instead of being confused about what's getting in your way. It has four elements that can help you diagnose your habit.

- *D is for Difficult*: This is where you find the task too hard. It could be because you lack the skills, experience, or confidence to tackle the task. Sometimes it can be all three! The concept of chewable chunks can come in handy by breaking the task down into simple-to-implement steps. Create a checklist of all the things that must be accomplished to complete the task and start on number one only.

  You will probably need to do some homework so that you begin to understand what the task entails. You can read a book, talk to an expert, watch videos, or do anything that helps flatten the learning curve.

- *U is for Unclear*: The task or assignment is not clearly defined. Make sure that if you are confused about a task you have been given to do, you ask questions. Clarify in detail what you are charged with doing and the expectations that come with the task (e.g., deadlines, outcomes, stakeholders, budget). This might sound simple, but a lot of people don't like asking questions because they might be seen as lacking the competencies needed. Don't fall into that trap. Have the courage to ask questions, and take careful notes you can review later. Clarity about the task is your goal. You need to see a pathway forward, or you will hesitate and procrastinate.

- *S is for Scary*: This could be fear of failure or success. Maybe you don't know where or how to start. This is where a thought partner comes in handy. They can help you think through what needs to be done and identify the possible roadblocks that might prevent your success. You can also get an accountability partner and make a strong commitment to starting the task as soon as possible. It's OK to be scared *and* to start the task anyway. Use meditation, deep breathing, specific and detailed visualization, or anything that helps you get started.

- *T is for Tedious*: Some things are just boring but still need to be done. This is where temptation bundling is very helpful. Pick something enjoyable that you can do alongside the tedious task. Remember the story of Dan Ariely, who paired watching great movies with giving himself a medication that made him ill. Remember chewable chunks, tiny steps and goals, and 10-minute dashes. Use your willpower strategically, usually at the beginning and the end of the task. Experiment with any technique to get started. Set up a nice reward for yourself upon completion of each small step, *not* at the very end. A tedious task just isn't any fun, so try anything that will get you through it.

36. I Want My Freedom

There are a fair number of procrastinators who fight the notion of building routines and habits or of using specific strategies to combat their procrastination. They don't want to "constrained' by these practices. They want to do things "their way." I call this the Sinatra syndrome, and it's a loser's game. You will need all of these ideas and more to manage your mean habit.

Just ask yourself, "How successful have I been dealing with my procrastination so far?" If you are comfortable with your progress and the quality of your life, then these ideas don't have any value for you. Keep on trucking!

But if you aren't happy with your progress or results, then get rid of the notion of "being free" and "doing it my way." Grow up. Procrastination is a crippling habit. Using any technique you can to manage it is the right, mature, and smart thing to do. It doesn't get better with wishful thinking, nor does it magically disappear all by itself.

37. Having a Bad Morning?

Sometimes we start our days with good intentions and high hopes, and then things just get screwy and disorganized. Nothing you try is working. I have these days less often than I did before, but every once in a while, I start to have a bad day. Around midmorning you feel defeated and see the day going downhill quickly, and you don't have any brakes.

This is a difficult place to be because you start to feel a little hopeless. You get overwhelmed, and the procrastination habit kicks in bigtime. How then do you save your day?

One of the most effective strategies when things start rolling downhill is to take a long break, say 30–60 minutes. You need to create some psychological distance from your current state of frustration by getting away from what you are struggling with. During this break, do some-thing physical: take a walk or a short run. You can also listen to music that you enjoy or read something interesting. The goal is to create a temporary break from your current psychological state.

After the healthy break, see if you can begin to turn things around. You might find that you have found a shift in perspective or a new insight about the task or a different way of tackling it. See the return to the task at hand as a new beginning.

Use strategies you have found effective in getting you to move forward—tackling something easy to experience a win, breaking off a chewable chunk and sticking with it for 10 minutes, reward a small success—whatever it might be. Anything that is doable and short-lived can change the direction of your day.

Once you get some positive momentum, you might find that your day gets turned around. I have found that this works about 50% of the time, so I think it's worth trying.

38. Are You a Lark or an Owl?

There is an interesting questionnaire on the website Sleephabits.net that takes about 10 minutes to fill out and will tell you if you are an owl or a lark. As you can imagine, the larks are morning people and the owls are afternoon or night people. Although the questionnaire is about sleep patterns, it is helpful in our context because it helps identify your energy sweet spot.

A lot of my clients are not early morning people whatsoever. Their energy doesn't kick in till noon or later. Many of the practices and pro-tocols suggested by productivity gurus involve starting really early—as early as 5:00 a.m.—and getting things done before everyone else shows up. This may work for some people, but not the owls.

Identifying your best time is important because that's when you want to practice focusing on the most important priorities of the day. For some that best time might be 7:00 a.m. For others it could be midafternoon.

The questionnaire gives you a score on a 1 to 5 scale. I found that I am a "moderately" morning type versus a "definite" morning type. This made real sense to me because I tried the "get up at five" routine for a week and was exhausted. Instead, I get up at six, read the paper, and then start my day easily. It works for me, and I am not trying to force myself to work hard at a time when I don't have the energy.

39. Go with the Flow

Mihaly Csiksentmihalyi (2008) is a famous and well-respected psychologist who wrote the bestseller *Flow: The Psychology of Optimal Experience*. He describes a psychological state in which we are completely immersed in a task or experience and often oblivious to outside distractions. This psychological "in the zone" experience is creative, enjoyable, and completely absorbing.

I haven't had many of these experiences, but when I have, it's usually been when I am very interested in a topic and learning something new. I remember working on a task and losing any sense of time. It's a wonderful experience. You might not get a flow experience very often, but if you do, don't stop! Go with it.

Throughout this book, I talk about using short work times, like 30 minutes (even less if that doesn't work for you), and then taking a break. But if you feel like you can continue after your designated time slot, keep moving. Use the flow to your advantage, because they don't happen all the time. Don't let your established schedule dictate your focus and energy. Go with it.

Chapter 5
The Procrastination Survey

The following survey has been informed by my reading of the research on procrastination (Combs, 2007; Steel, 2011; Fiore, 2007; Ferrari, 2010) and my actual experience of procrastination, along with hundreds of conversations with leaders who deal with their own procrastination every day.

People who have taken this survey have found it to be commonsensical, practical, and informative. Understanding the severity of your procrastination can be a helpful guide toward managing it. If you do an item analysis and identify the specific statements where your scores are the highest, you might gain insight into where your real challenges lie.

Please don't overthink this informal survey. Use your natural instincts and give each statement an honest score. Stay away from giving a lot of threes (3), which is a neutral score. Having lots of threes won't be very helpful in assessing your tendency to procrastinate.

Do *not* use the results of the survey to be self-critical or beat yourself up. It is simply not helpful. The goal is to get a snapshot of your procrastination habit so that you can create processes and protocols to help manage it. This is an educational tool, not an opportunity to criticize yourself.

I suggest that you have a friend or colleague who knows you well take the survey *about* you. This way you will have a reality check to compare your own answers to. Your friends and colleagues see you in action every day and can add a helpful perspective. Almost always, people who have asked a friend or colleague to fill out the survey about them have found the conversation to be value added. This will take a little courage, but it is well worth the investment.

If you want a validated survey, please consider Tuckman's (1991) because you will have faith in its rigor and results. For those who want an informal but informative snapshot of their tendency to procrastinate, this will serve you quite well.

After you score the statements, I will provide some advice on how to interpret the scores as well as some strategies to utilize when managing your procrastination. Enjoy the learning journey!

Please use the following scale when answering the set of statements:

1: extremely uncharacteristic

2: moderately uncharacteristic

3: neutral

4: moderately characteristic

5: extremely characteristic

1. Paying my bills on time is often a real challenge.

1   2   3   4   5

2. I really dislike waiting in line for things.

1   2   3   4   5

3. If I am honest, I often tell myself, "I'll do this tomorrow," when faced with a difficult task or assignment.

    1   2   3   4   5

4. For the most part, I return phone calls and emails promptly.

    1   2   3   4   5

5. I often find myself rushing around to attend meetings on time, get to the airport on time, or commute to work on time. I am often late for these events.

    1   2   3   4   5

6. I usually wait until the last minute to do important things (e.g., pay my income taxes, balance my family budget, or write a report).

    1   2   3   4   5

7. I tend to underestimate how long important assignments will take.

    1   2   3   4   5

8. I often find myself delaying doing simple things, even when I know they will only take a few minutes.

    1   2   3   4   5

9. When I am working, I often get distracted by surfing the internet, playing video games, or checking Facebook and LinkedIn.

    1   2   3   4   5

10. I usually find it very challenging to start an important assignment, task, or project.

    1   2   3   4   5

11. My best friends would describe me as easily distractable.

    1   2   3   4   5

12. I often find myself overwhelmed by the many things I need to do.

    1   2   3   4   5

13. I feel a fair amount of guilt for not completing important tasks.

    1   2   3   4   5

14. At the end of the day, I often feel regret for not getting done what I was supposed to accomplish.

    1   2   3   4   5

15. I have tried to use some time management techniques (e.g., writing a to-do list or breaking down big tasks into smaller steps), but they just don't seem to work for me.

    1   2   3   4   5

16. If there is something difficult to do, or I'm not sure how to do it, I often put it off until later.

    1   2   3   4   5

17. I find myself delaying making important decisions, even when I know that time is running out.

    1   2   3   4   5

18. I often wait until the last minute to finish a project.

    1   2   3   4   5

19. I often wait until I feel inspired or motivated to tackle an assignment.

    1   2   3   4   5

20. I often find myself being overcommitted and say yes to too many things.

    1   2   3   4   5

How to Score the Survey

There are a total of 20 statements, and the most you can score is 100 points. Just add the scores you gave each statement to arrive at a total score.

Any score below 50 indicates you are a mild procrastinator and there isn't much to worry about. Many people score in this range.

Scores between 50 and 75 indicate that you are migrating toward being a real procrastinator.

Scores above 75 qualify you as a professional procrastinator!

No matter what your score is, I suggest that you do a careful item analysis. Pay attention to the statements you marked with a 4 or, especially, a 5. There might only be a handful of these, but they will focus your attention on what you need to work on.

Consider item 5, "I often find myself rushing around." If you scored yourself highly here, you might consider implementing a protocol that supports you leaving for work at least 15 minutes earlier than usual. Or perhaps you could manage your calendar differently, not scheduling back-to-back meetings. Or when traveling, you can go to the airport at least one hour earlier than normal.

I personally have implemented this extra hour of airport time, because I nearly missed two flights due to unexpected traffic jams. I was stressed like crazy and told myself that rushing to the airport was stupid. Now, I almost always get to the airport at least two hours before my flight That way, I can read the newspaper, organize my agenda for the day, drink a latte (my favorite), and, most importantly, relax before my flight.

Or consider item 9, "When I am working, I often get distracted by surfing the internet, playing video games, or checking Facebook and LinkedIn." You might have to find a quiet place that is distraction-free for an hour each day to focus on your priority of the day. This will take some discipline, but it is an effective and powerful practice to implement. Distractions are everywhere. They are one of the most difficult things to deal with, and are often the number one reason people procrastinate.

You will find scores of practical ideas and strategies in this book that will be helpful in managing your procrastination. But here's the thing: this will be a very hard journey to undertake. It is essential that you try to focus on one thing to improve—not several things, just *one thing*. Procrastinators are famous for tackling the whole mess at once and failing miserably. Keep this mantra in mind: "Focus on one thing."

For example, you might try to be distraction-free for one hour a day. This would be an enormous accomplishment for any procrastinator and could be a game changer *if* you can actually use the distraction-free time to focus your attention and accomplish something.

Remember: focus on one thing, and it will make an appreciable difference.

Chapter 6
Mini Chapters

The following mini chapters are topic-specific quick reads that offer practical tools and advice. They are tailored for procrastinators who often—not always—want to "get it" quickly and want something actionable and uncomplicated.

- *How to Say No to Others*—Procrastinators often find it hard to say no. This mini chapter shows you how to do so politely and effectively.

- *The Big Ten Procrastination Strategies*—You can get overwhelmed by way too many tips and strategies for managing your procrastination habit. This mini chapter provides just 10 of the very best.

- *The Procrastination Strategy Matrix*—This matrix organizes information around what kind of procrastination you engage in most of the time and offers specific strategies to deal with your specific style. This is a helpful diagnostic and can help you create a game plan going forward.

- *Small Wisdoms*—Some small ideas can have big results if operationalized. The ideas presented in this mini chapter have been gleaned from years of mistakes and mishaps, successes and accomplishments. Many of my clients and fellow procrastinators have shared some for your consideration

Mini Chapter 1: How to Say No to Others

We let people steal our time like we have an unlimited amount.

—Seneca

For years I was usually overwhelmed with all the work I was and was not doing. A trusted colleague said to me, "I know what your problem is."

I was stunned that she thought that I had a problem. I actually didn't want to hear about it, but because she was a good friend, I said, "Oh really? What's my problem?"

"You don't know how to say no."

"What do you mean?" I asked incredulously.

"You are a soft touch. If you think about it, you are doing everyone else's work, but not your own."

I didn't like to hear what she said, but she was right. I was very busy, which doesn't look like procrastination at first glance but is often a hidden form of it. I didn't like my workload and responsibilities, and I like to help people, so I said yes way too often. I was well liked, *and* I didn't get my stuff done.

Over the years, I have witnessed this habit of being "nice." When I ask people about it, almost always they admit that they are avoiding work by saying yes way too often. We do this because we are nice people, want to be kind, want to help others, or want to be liked. It's also a way for us to avoid doing our own work.

The problem with saying yes too often is that you are saying no to other opportunities in your life and creating more work for yourself. You don't need more work to do; you need to do *your* work. Remember that procrastinators love distractions. Saying yes is a great distraction that takes you away from your work.

I first encountered this dynamic of saying yes to others many years ago as I was coaching a senior leader who was overwhelmed almost all the time. I spent a couple of days with him so that I could better understand his workload and style. I was soon struck by how often people reached out to him for help, advice, and support, and how often he said yes to their requests. It was no wonder he was overwhelmed—he was helping others with *their* work while trying ineffectively to do his own work. I realized that he just couldn't say no to others. More importantly, he didn't know how.

I began to be very interested in how to say no, both for myself and for my client, and went on a learning journey. The big revelation for me was that by not saying no, my client was engaging in a subtle, counterintuitive form of procrastination and self-sabotage.

The following suggestions come from my experience with lots of leaders who engage in this interesting habit. I hope you find them useful.

Learning to say no effectively can be one of the best time-savers around. It can help boost your productivity because you will have time to work on *your* priorities. But learning to say no to others is not easy unless you tend to be a cantankerous or angry person.

You need to be very clear about who you want to say yes to. This could be family, close friends, or bosses. Keep the list as short as possible, because if it's too long, it won't really matter. The relational stakes are much higher with a short list of important people. With these individuals, you can still use some of the strategies that follow if you need to, but most of us will find that challenging.

Another strong suggestion—and this goes for your important people as well as others—*never* respond in the moment unless it's an emergency. Tell people you will consider their request and get back to them reasonably soon with an answer. People who make a lot of requests of others know how difficult it is to say no. You need to create some psychological distance before responding. You are not obligated to give them a response immediately. Never forget this.

Strategy 1: Rehearse Your Responses

You have to practice saying no to others. Most adults are uncomfortable with role-playing or "behavioral rehearsal," but it's an important tool for building a repertoire of responses when confronted with a request.

You can practice with a spouse, partner, or close friend. Monitor your emotional response to saying no. You might find that your initial response is a guilty feeling. Perhaps you're fearful of disappointing someone or just plain uncomfortable. That's natural and OK. Get used to the feelings before the actual requests start inevitably coming your way.

It's almost always helpful to have a handful of respectful responses prepared for when someone makes a request. Here's one: "Thanks for thinking about me. Let me get back to you about this. Once I review my schedule, I will make sure I follow up with you."

This response allows you to create the psychological distance you need to provide a thoughtful, not knee-jerk, response in the moment. Always follow up as promised, especially if you are turning down the request, because it maintains your integrity and is respectful.

Using this strategy gives you the time to review your schedule and determine if this request fits into your personal or professional interests and goals. If it doesn't, then say no politely—preferably by phone, because it's easier to say no that way. For example, "I've looked at my workload and responsibilities very carefully, and although I would like to help, I cannot at this time."

Stand firm. There is a very good chance the requestor will ask again, so be ready for it. "I would like to be helpful, but I simply can't." Remember, firmness and politeness are keys to these responses. Practice, practice, practice.

Strategy 2: Provide Them with an Option if You Can

If you can't help the requestor personally, you might know of a person, organization, or resource that would be helpful for them to consider. Share this information with them *after* you have declined their offer. For example, "I know that Jim Seitz knows a lot about this subject. He might be willing to help you with this. I can give you his contact information, and you can tell him I made the referral."

Do *not* call Jim and try to make a match. Let the requestor do their own legwork.

Another example: "I know the World Economic Forum is a great resource for what you want to write about. Consider visiting their web portal and doing some research there." Or "I've heard of a local organization that uses college students to help move furniture. They are supposed to be pretty cheap and responsible. Here's their phone number."

You get the idea. Help the requestor a little with a suggested next step, but don't do the work for them. Bottom line: if you can be helpful, do it.

Saying No to Your Boss

There are plenty of times when your boss will make a surprise, even unreasonable request. You need to have a strategy in place so you can give them a gentle no.

The essential question you need to ask in this situation is, what kind of relationship do you have with your boss? If it is a constructive relationship and you have some credibility with them, the following strategy will almost always be effective. If the relationship is strained or your boss is a jerk, then the chances of success are limited. Still, it's worth a try.

Often, bosses make requests without much understanding of employees' current workloads and responsibilities. This doesn't mean they don't care; it's often just the way it is. When they make a request, they usually believe you have both the time and capacity to handle it.

One possible scenario will give you a picture of what a gentle no looks like. "This new assignment sounds interesting [*or* challenging, *or* really big], and I am very open to discussing it with you. But [*yes, you say* but] I need your advice and help in figuring out how it could fit into my already full workload. If this is a top priority for you, then I need to discuss how I can reprioritize my work assignments so that I can create the space and time to take this new assignment on."

You get the idea. You are not rejecting the new assignment, you are seeking their support in thinking through your workload responsibilities. Almost always, with a *reasonable* boss, they will be open to this conversation because you have credibility with them. Credibility is key.

Walk your boss through your top-priority assignments and responsibilities. Don't cover everything, because they will lose interest quickly and you will look like a complainer. Highlight the big stuff and provide a ballpark notion of the time commitments these top priorities take.

Often, the boss will realize that your plate is full and they need to create space for the new assignment. The two of you are working together as thought partners, solving the problem jointly. You might find that a certain assignment can be delayed or delegated to someone else.

When I have used this process with my clients, many have reported that their boss had a better understanding, even a revelation of sorts, about how full the employee's plate was. This is a good thing.

After you have reprioritized, delayed, or delegated assignments, you need to discuss the implications of the new assignment *before* you take it on. Some questions to talk over are:

- What's the desired outcome of this assignment? What does success look like?

- What resources will be needed (e.g., people, money, space, technology, expertise, consultants)?

- What are the challenges and barriers to success that we can identify (e.g., political tensions, lack of experience, work groups in other parts of the organization, union problems). This might be the most important question because, as we say, "The mud pies are out there waiting." You need to identify them *before* stepping in them, and create effective strategies to manage them.

- What are the realistic time frames? What are the deadlines and mini deadlines? Often this needs some negotiation because bosses forget that projects usually take longer than anticipated.

- What does the communication process look like? Will it be via face-to-face meetins, email, Zoom? Will it be monthly, weekly, daily?

- What will the problem-solving process look like? Problems are guaranteed so you want to establish a problem-solving protocol up front, before you begin the assignment. The thing you want to hear from your boss is some version of "When you begin to feel overwhelmed or stuck, I want to hear about the problem right away. If I can help solve it early in the game, that's my preference. I don't want to deal with a slow-growing crisis ever." Think through a commonsensical process for dealing with the inevitable problems that will emerge.

Depersonalize the No

Lastly, it is very important to depersonalize a request. Realize that when you say no to a person, you are *not* rejecting the individual personally. You are saying no to the "opportunity" that has been presented.

This is an important notion. It can help you avoid the guilt, resentment, and personal obligation that can kick in immediately after a request is made. You are not turning down the person; you are turning down the request.

Procrastination Note

Lazy people are usually very smart individuals who realize it's hard for most people to refuse a request—that's why they are good at asking. Lazy people rarely feel guilty about asking others for help. Never forget this. Procrastinators are different, because we are often consumed with guilt. Lazy people have learned that if they pick the people who are busy and get things done, they have an ideal victim. So be ready for them with a no!

Suggested Resources

The Power of a Positive No by William Ury is a great book about the relational dynamics of saying no to requests respectfully—and saying yes to yourself.

Essentialism by Greg McKean provides some excellent advice on how to say no respectfully, especially to your boss.

> A No uttered from the deepest conviction is better than and greater than a yes merely uttered to please or worse to avoid trouble.
>
> —Mahatma Gandhi

Mini Chapter 2:
The Big Ten Procrastination Strategies

There are whole lot of things you can do to manage the procrastination habit. I have shared about 100 in this book. I have highlighted the ones I think are really effective and worth consideration. I don't want to overwhelm you with too many good ideas, so this mini chapter suggests a few to focus on and think through to see if they fit for you. Once again, this is a key theme throughout the book—pick things that *feel* right or *resonate* with you.

Starting Is the Key Strategy

Starting is the first step in breaking the procrastination habit. Do anything that creates action of some kind—anything. Use routines, chewable chunks, or visualization of the completion of a small task. Often, after a few minutes, two things happen: (a) the task doesn't seem as noxious and overwhelming, and (b) you feel some momentum to continue doing the task you were avoiding.

Rewards Work

Rewards work, so use them. Use a lot of them. Don't fall into the mental trap that tells you, "I *shouldn't* need to reward myself." It's self-sabotage and simply not useful. This is a twofer: get "shouldn'ts" out of your life!

Be Kind to Yourself

Procrastinators tend to be self-critical and even mean to themselves. It isn't helpful. It's hurtful and will keep you trapped in your procrastination habit, feeling guilty, stressed, and incompetent. Think about how you would treat a friend who had this habit. You would be understanding and supportive. You would help them manage their habit. You wouldn't criticize them or make them feel even worse about themselves.

Distractions Kill Our Attention

You can get caught up in a lot of debates about distractions and that you "should" be able to ignore them. We live in an extraordinarily distracting world. Many of our electronic devices and social media have been *designed* to be addictive. You are fighting a losing battle, in my view. Remember, willpower is a very limited resource.

If our environment is distracting, we need to change it. There are a lot of strategies in the book that talk about this, but three things are key.

- Physically go somewhere that has no distractions.

- Put your smartphone out of reach, like in another room.

- Turn off all notifications on your devices that keep ringing and dinging for your attention.

Chewable Chunks Are the Way to Go

Always think about how you can break a large or noxious task you are avoiding into small, doable tasks that are manageable in limited time frames—say, 10 minutes. This could mean creating a rough outline of a project, cleaning one corner of your desk, or organizing one folder on your computer. Start small to achieve big.

Make Your Progress Visible

Every sport has a scorecard, so they know who won or lost the game. Create some kind of visual reminder of your progress and place it in full view in your work space. There are many strategies for capturing this information. You could use a checklist where you check things off as you accomplish your tasks. A whiteboard allows you to erase each task on your list, so you can see the list getting smaller. Use whatever works for you, and mark your progress. It's a motivator.

Setbacks Are Inevitable, so Plan for Them

Almost everything meaningful takes longer and is harder than we imagined. This can be a curse for procrastinators. We can get overwhelmed before we begin. Or we might get stuck in the middle and lose hope that we can finish.

Setbacks will occur on the journey to accomplishment, so think about them. *Use the pre mortem technique* before you start a project. Ask a thought partner to help. When you have identified the potential mud pies, think about how you can manage them. There will still be mud pies waiting, but you will have effective strategies for dealing with most of them.

Secondly—and this takes courage and discipline—seek the lessons from your setbacks. There are reasons why hurdles appear. Most important are your reactions to them. When things go wrong, we can get demotivated quickly and put things off, and the cycle of avoidance continues. Use these blips to learn about yourself. Journal about what you are thinking and feeling. You will probably find patterns that kick in when you experience a hurdle. Identifying the patterns can provide insight and a possible way out of the situation.

Have Fewer Goals

Many procrastinators are ambitious and way too aspirational about what can actually be accomplished. "Less is more" is the mantra of winners. Try mightily to figure out what really matters to you, and create realistic plans for achieving that. This will be really hard to accomplish, but it's the path to success.

There are too many "experts" and "successful" people, mostly billionaires, who tell us to think 10 times bigger that we imagine, so that our dreams are larger than life. If that fits your picture of reality, go for it. But most of us won't be billionaires or all-star athletes. For us, let's define what really matters and go for it. Let's not set ourselves up for failure from the very beginning.

Use Your Willpower Strategically

Willpower is a limited resource, much like a muscle that tires after use. Given its limitations, we need to use it when it matters. For many procrastinators, this is at the beginning of a task. For others, including me, it's near the end, or the "last mile." Try to figure out when you need it, and then apply it. Don't think it's an endless resource you can access at any time.

Also, forget the stories of world-class athletes and SEAL Team Six. They are aberrations—they might be positive ones, but they're unrealistic models. They train full-time to do what they do, and they have lots of coaching and strong support from team members. They have a finite amount of willpower just like you do; it only looks different.

Multitasking Is Killing Your Productivity and Feeding Your Procrastination Habit

The great seduction of multitasking is that it feels productive. Unfortunately it isn't. The research is overwhelming on this point. If you can focus on only one thing and get rid of distractions, you will accomplish more and not feed the procrastination habit. This will not be easy, but it's a game changer.

> Think of many things; do one.
> —*Portuguese Proverb*

Mini Chapter 3:
A Diagnostic Tool for Procrastination

> Motivation follows action. Get started and you'll find
> that motivation follows.
> —Timothy Pychyl

Joseph Ferrari (2010) is a psychologist and academic at DePaul University. His book, *Still Procrastinating: The No Regrets Guide to Getting It Done* is a good read with helpful information on the topic. He identifies five big reasons why we procrastinate. His list is a variation on the DUST model discussed in chapter 4. Although it's not an exhaustive list, it's a good starting point to think about how and why we procrastinate, along with some effective strategies for neutralizing the five challenges he identifies.

You can use Ferrari's five reasons as a beginning framework for a more comprehensive diagnostic scan of your current procrastination habit. Then think about implementing some of the suggested strategies to deal with them. You might find that you have more than one reason, so you might have to try multiple strategies.

For example, you might find that you are feeling distracted *and* not very creative. This is a tough combination, but he offers practical ideas for breaking through both these barriers.

Feeling Overwhelmed

This is a big theme throughout my book. Here are some ways of dealing with this challenge.

- When the overwhelmed feeling begins, take three deep, slow breaths. This might lessen the intensity of the feeling and allow you to push forward.

- Think about chewable chunks and not the entire task. Break it down into smaller parts and focus *only* on the next step, not the whole thing. Make sure you have a reward system in place before you start the smaller tasks.

- Talk with a thought partner about your plans to tackle the task and what a realistic schedule for completing it might be. Remember, procrastinators aren't very good at estimating how long something will take. Getting a reality check is helpful.

Getting Distracted

Again, distraction is a big theme in my book because procrastinators tend to be distraction machines. Some strategies:

- Go someplace quiet. If your current environment is messy, noisy, and busy, go someplace else. This will not be easy to do at first, but it's one of the most effective strategies you can implement.

- Work in 10-minute sprints or dashes. Try to hunker down, set a timer, and see what you can get done in 10 minutes. Make sure you have a nice little reward at the end of the 10 minutes, but stay away from social media. At the end of the first sprint, check in with yourself and see if you want to or can continue for another 10 minutes. About 50% of the time, you will find that you can. If you can't, it's not a big deal; you have experienced success already.

- Turn off all email and social media bells and whistles. Those little noises are like attention magnets. Once again, try for 10 minutes and see what happens. Refer to the "Toolbox" appendix for some suggestions of great apps to use to block out social media and email.

- Put your smartphone in another room so you can't hear or see it. Create a situation in which it will take you conscious effort to get to the phone. This will be a real challenge for many of us because we can become anxious when we don't have our phones. Don't just turn the phone off. You will still be looking at it, curious about what's going on in the wider world. Moving the phone to another room forces you to make a conscious effort to retrieve it, and might slow you down a little.

- Learn to meditate. If you can build a meditation practice for just 10 minutes a day, you will improve your mindfulness and focus.

Despising the Task

This is a big one for me personally. It's very difficult to work on something you intensely dislike. But we have to do it anyway. Some strategies:

- Consider temptation bundling—combining something pleasant, like listening to music, with the noxious task. Remember the powerful story of Dan Ariely, the psychologist who was prescribed the drug Interferon. It made him very sick, so he watched his favorite movies while experiencing the terrible effects of the drug.

- Get an accountability partner, who is someone you respect and know very well. Both of those qualities need to be present in your partner in order for this technique to work. Make a commitment to this person that you will achieve a goal—e.g., apply for a driver's license, go to graduate school, or finish a report—and keep your word. If you truly respect this person, you will be very reluctant to go back on your word. Use this for truly important things, because there is real relationship risk attached to this.

- Pawn it! This is an unusual and effective strategy to employ for really important tasks you are procrastinating on. Give a friend, business associate, or partner something you really value, such as your engagement ring or a pair of cufflinks your father gifted to you. Have them hold the item until you have completed the task. Obviously, this is a very serious strategy to consider, especially if you give the item to someone you know won't return it until all conditions are met!

- Chewable chunks are another way to go with this challenge. With tasks we despise, we often think about the whole salami. Slice that salami into little tasks, build rewards along the way, and gut it out in small chunks of time.

- Lastly, try to see a connection between what you despise and your higher goals and purpose. If you can see how the current task brings you closer to your aspirations, it might motivate you to tough it out. Often, it's difficult to see the connection. This is where you might need a thought partner to push your thinking, reveal a different way to get it done, or open up a blind spot you are unaware of. Using thought partners is almost always a smart thing to do when procrastinating.

Lacking Confidence

Often people procrastinate about something because they don't know much about the task, haven't had much experience with it, or don't know how to begin. Consider the following:

- You might have to build your knowledge about a specific topic or practice. You can watch a YouTube video (something I do regularly) or a TED Talk. You can take a course about the subject. Talk to someone who has completed the same task. They will often make great suggestions on how to learn faster. Bottom line, be willing to ask others for help. If you build your skill, you will often build your courage and your confidence.

- Watch your self-talk, because it can stop you dead in your tracks. Thoughts like *I'm not smart enough* or *I am going to look stupid* or *This is just way too hard* won't get you anywhere. Be mindful of the messages you are giving yourself. Instead, use more positive self-talk, like *I choose to do this task* or *I am going to learn a lot on this project.*

- Watch your expectations about the task. If this is the first time you have tackled the topic, you will have some struggles. This is *inevitable*. It is part of your learning journey. It's not a bad thing; it's just the way it is. How can you know something you have never done before? There is a learning curve at the beginning of new tasks. It's normal, so be realistic about what's possible.

- Use a thought partner to help you think about how to start the learning process (e.g., take a course, talk with an expert, read several articles). Confidence is highly dependent on how we see success. Who wants to start project that they believe they will fail at? That's why having a *realistic* plan moving forward is essential. The plan, if well thought out, will be a road map to success. You don't want to wing it and just plow forward. Get help, create a plan, and build in mini deadlines and a reward system.

- Lastly, really specific visualization can be very helpful. I describe the visualization process in chapter 3. When you lack confidence about something, having a clear, detailed picture of what success looks like is a smart thing to do

Blocking Creativity

There are times when we just get blocked psychologically and can't see any path forward or possible solution. This can be frustrating and can kick the procrastination habit into high gear.

- Step away from the task and do something active, like dancing, walking, running, or cleaning. Often when people are immersed in a physical activity, creative ideas and alternatives just pop into their heads. You are not focusing on the task at hand, and this gives you some psychological distance from it. I have a colleague who takes a long, hot shower when they get stymied. It helps them relax, it feels good, and sometimes they see something about the challenge they hadn't seen before.

- Seek out a thought partner—someone who thinks differently than you do and can provide a perspective you currently don't have. They can see things you can't. This has nothing to do with how smart you are. It's just that we all have blind spots that we just can't see. Others can reveal these blind spots by offering different approaches and options. One caution: you need to be conscious about "comfortable cloning," which describes choosing a thought partner who thinks just like you do. They might have the same job experience, educational background, ethnicity, gender, and so on. We choose these "clones" because they are comfortable for us. Consciously seek out thought partners who see differently. It can be an effective strategy for getting unjammed and moving forward.

- Learn some creativity practices like brainstorming, metaphorical problem-solving, or brain-writing. There are hundreds of tools, techniques, and practices you can learn to use that will boost your creative IQ.

Mini Chapter 4: Small Wisdoms

Little things a can make a difference. Some things to consider:

- Try to not work in your bedroom if you can avoid it. There are way too many distractions, and you can always find a reason to take a nap and avoid work.

- Finishing is really hard for many procrastinators. It's frustrating because most of the work is already done—but not all of it, and that's what matters. Finishing is where I experience my biggest challenges, so I have to have many strategies in place to help me finish well. For me, the last mile is the longest one, so I prepare for it. I use as many strategies as possible—whatever works to gain completion and feel accomplished.

- Use visualization techniques, because they work. There are hundreds of books and articles about the power of visualization. Learn about it and do it often. Picture your success, especially with the small things, because they can add up over time. World-class athletes swear by the power of visualization, and it can work for procrastinators

- It's better to do something than nothing. I've previously mentioned "constructive" procrastination. Using this technique, you get something done. It might not be a high-level priority, but you at least get *something* done. That's a good thing. You can't always work on the top-priority things, so have some meaningful lower-priority things that are easier to accomplish on a to-do list in your back pocket.

- You always have to expect setbacks, because they are going to happen. Use the pre mortem technique to anticipate possible blocks and plan for them if you can. This is where a thought partner comes in real handy. When the setbacks occur, don't beat yourself up about them. That's self-sabotage. It hurts you and doesn't make a difference or improve anything. If you can, try to learn from the setback. This will not be easy because we tend to avoid looking at our mistakes and failures. But take courage and strive to do it. As the Dalai Lama said, "*When you lose, don't lose the lesson.*" Success and failure both leave clues, so search for them if you can. Again, think about using a thought partner when exploring a setback. They are not psychologically invested in the situation, so they can be subjective about it. They can also provide support going forward

- Deadlines either work or they don't. Try them and see what happens. There is a mixed bag of research that indicates why they work for some people and not others. If you have a deadline that's a long way off, create mini deadlines with milestones (e.g., choose a paint color by Friday, get painting supplies on Saturday, paint the trim on Sunday), so you can see the path forward.

- Motivation follows action, *not* the other way around. That might seem counterintuitive—it was for me—but waiting to feel motivated is usually not helpful, especially for procrastinators. Timothy Pychyl, who is an expert on procrastination, taught me this concept. One of his primary findings is that simply getting started can lead to feelings of motivation. Quit waiting for it, because it ain't coming. Just do something.

- Attention is like a sponge: it can only hold so much at a time. That's why it's important to take breaks throughout your workday. It can energize you, reward you, and build more absorptive capacity to keep you focused on the task at hand.

- Starting is the hardest part for most procrastinators. That's where we get stuck, so strategize on *how to get started*. Things like routines, rituals, working in a group, small steps, and rewards are all helpful things to try.

- Distractions are usually interesting, even fun. That's why they are the enemy. Never forget this. Do whatever you can to create a distraction-free space. This may mean wearing noise-canceling headphones, going somewhere quiet, or installing blocking apps to quiet all the noises from your smartphone and computer. If it's quiet, then at least you have a chance of moving things forward.

- We tend to be impatient and want to see immediate results. This is part of the powerful and negative dynamic we live in. We want instant results, which is a loser's game. Our procrastination habit didn't just appear overnight. It's been around for a long time. It's ingrained in our brains. Patience with yourself is a strategic wedge and will, over time, prove to be powerful. Mindfulness and meditation may be helpful. If you can quiet your mind a little, the impulsiveness and impatience may dissipate somewhat.

- You are not lazy. Lazy people don't have any guilt about their habit; it's just the way they are. Procrastinators usually have *lots* of guilt that shadows our day. If you work diligently on creating new routines, practicing self-compassion, and learning to focus on the most important things in your life, you will feel less guilty and enjoy life more.

- Learn to meditate, if only for a few minutes each day. It is one of the most effective and powerful things you can do to change your procrastination habit. It will help you become more mindful and aware of your thoughts and feelings. You learn to realize that you can have thoughts and feelings *and not act on them.* Powerful feelings and emotions are almost always present. You can choose to pay attention to them, experience avoidance, and start to procrastinate. Or you can simply observe them and not do anything. This will be very hard and will take some time, but meditation is *the* game-changer for managing your procrastination habit.

- Small things can become big things over time, which is counterintuitive for many of us. We want to hit home runs instead of singles. Procrastinators often want to see big results fast. This is another part of the negative dynamic of this habit. If you can focus on small wins, you can see results *over time.* For example, when I sought to lose weight, I talked to my doctor. He has known me for many years and understands my sense of urgency and results-orientation. I told him I want to lose 10 pounds in the next month. He suggested that I focus on losing one pound a week. In two months, ideally, I would lose eight pounds in a healthy way. I resisted the advice initially, but then agreed to try it. I successfully lost the eight pounds in two months without any dramatic change in my lifestyle—and I will probably keep it off. Note: many procrastinators want *dramatic* change and bite off more than they can chew. Then they fail at their goal. Think about the small things that can matter, because that's the way out of a habit.

- Learn to ask for help. This sounds simple, but a lot of procrastinators find it hard. If you feel stuck with a task, talk to someone about it. They might have a different perspective about how to approach the task and might be willing to help you jump-start a process. I had one friend who procrastinated about organizing his garage for five years! He was bold enough to ask a friendly neighbors for help. The deal they made was a swap: after my friend's garage was organized, he would help his neighbor clean his garage. Both garages got cleaned because one of them was willing to ask for help. You don't have to do everything by yourself.

- When we get tired, we tend to procrastinate more. Roy Baumeister, an expert on procrastination, advises us to remember this. If we haven't gotten enough sleep the night before, our tendency to procrastinate will loom large. So if you are tired, you might not be able to tackle a tough task. Do something easier, so that you accomplish something. I'm not trying to supply you with an excuse to procrastinate; I'm just being realistic. If you can take a nap and wake from it refreshed, then do that (it doesn't work for me).

Appendices

Appendix 1
My Schedule (Ideally)

The following describes how I manage my professional time and productivity as a procrastinator. It took a long time to figure this process out, with a lot of frustration, fumbling, and experimentation. I am faithful to it about 90% of the time, which is pretty good.

I work at home when I am not traveling, so I have a lot of freedom to design my schedule, to-do lists, and priorities to focus on. I don't take this for granted. realize that I have a lot of privilege. Nor am I suggesting that you organize yourself this way. I just wanted to share what works for me after years of research and practice.

I use 30-minute chunks of time with 10-minute breaks in between. I tried 60 minutes initially, but it didn't work for me. Sixty minutes was too long for me to be focused on what I was doing.

This is an important point: you have to craft your work routine and schedule to fit your personality and work style. It might take a significant time investment to figure it out; it took me over a year. I still procrastinate at times, but overall, I do pretty well.

I get up at 6:00 a.m. every day, make coffee, get a bite to eat and read the *Philadelphia Inquirer*, my regional paper. I love reading the newspaper first thing in the morning because it grounds me and helps me feel informed as I begin my day.

I know there are some productivity gurus who tell us to rise early—say five o'clock—and write in a journal, meditate, and exercise. They recommend not paying attention to the news because it is "distracting."

I tried this for a week and hated it. You have to design a schedule that works for you. Don't try to force it. Everyone is different.

My professional goal is to work for five good hours every day except Sundays. I take short breaks during the day to relax, renew, refresh—and nibble on some food.

I try hard not to do social media during these breaks, because it is never only 10 minutes. I did this at first and found myself mesmerized by a lot of useless but interesting information. I lost track of time. My particular attention addiction is watching the stock market, because I invest most of my money in it. As you can predict, when I am winning, the day goes great. When I am losing, it's not so great. I have to be very disciplined about how much time I spend watching the stock news, and it's very difficult

Initially, I tried to do eight work hours of focused work daily, but it was just too much time to concentrate and be productive. I naturally migrated to five really productive hours a day. It doesn't feel forced. In total, I work more than five hours, but in terms of high-priority focused work, I limit myself to five hours. For the rest of the day, I do secondary things.

I mark my progress in 30-minute increments because I find I can usually do a good 30 minutes of work before my mind begins to wander. My accomplishments list looks like this at the beginning of the day:

30   30   30   30   30

30   30   30   30   30

I write it in really big numerals on a whiteboard *across* the room. Then I start a timer. When it goes off, I *get out of my chair*, go over to the whiteboard, and cross out a 30 with a red marker. I really like the feeling of crossing it out. The reason I put the list across the room is that the physical movement of walking to it gives me a nice sensation of accomplishing something—might sound weird, but it works for me.

If I am doing a writing day, I try to keep to the five-hour schedule, but I also mark the number of pages I have written. I could easily dawdle my time away with writing and rewriting the same page, searching for perfection, so noting the number of written pages is very important. It's helpful to have a process or an outcome measure—and sometimes you need both.

I don't judge the quality of the pages I write as I do my rough draft. I just produce as much as I can. After I have finished a certain number of pages, I do a pretty careful edit of my draft. This is an important idea for writers or people who write reports for work: I *separate* my writing from my editing.

There is a great little book, *The Artful Edit: On the Practice of Editing Yourself*, by Susan Bell (2008). It helped me to dramatically change my writing habits. I used to combine writing with editing, and it was a slow and dreadful process.

When I finish a chapter or complete a report for a client, I put the title on a big yellow sheet of paper. It helps me remember what I have accomplished. Remember, visual reminders are very helpful.

My work day starts around eight o'clock in the morning. I am not rigid with my starting time because I know I will put in five hours of priority work whenever I start. There are some productivity experts who insist on starting each day at a specific time and establishing a routine that way. I have lots of routines I follow, but not with starting times.

In the late afternoon, from about four o'clock until five thirty or so, I usually return emails, make phone calls, and do the kind of work that won't take too much time, thinking, or effort. This might include light research for a project, outlining an article, or writing a letter to a client.

I have been able to accustom most of my clients to the idea that the two hours from 3:00 p.m. to 5:00 p.m. are when I am available for Zoom meetings, phone calls, and regular meetings in my office. This works about 80% of the time. I have to be responsive to their needs also, so I will take time between eight and three if necessary to respond to my clients.

I have found that if I write or do research for an hour, then make some phone calls, then go back to my writing for a while, and then have a Zoom meeting, it messes my day up. I never really gain momentum or feel like I am accomplishing things. So I try to focus on my work between eight and three, and not allow interruptions during the day.

I'm strict about the five hours of focused work from Monday through Thursday. On Fridays I am very flexible with my schedule. I do some focused work on secondary priorities. I also return phone calls, respond to important emails, conduct correspondence, and review emerging opportunities. This might be a lunch meeting with a client or watching a webinar. I also use my Fridays to bundle my errands. I like the flexibility of running errands in the off-hours and avoiding long lines.

I also do a five hour work day on most Saturdays unless I have a personal obligation of some kind (e.g., wedding, charity function, visiting friends). On Sundays I relax a lot. I watch Sunday morning TV shows, read the paper, and dawdle around a lot. I usually go for a long walk, often with a friend, and have an early dinner to top off the day.

The key theme here is this is a schedule I have created that works for me. It might not work for you. Create something that feels right and plays to your productivity style, procrastination habits, and time-management sensibilities.

There are a few embedded themes in my schedule that deserve highlighting:

- I get up at the same time every day.

- I follow a morning routine that is pleasurable and informative.

- I can be focused for 30 minutes.

- I make my progress visible and physical.

- I take breaks throughout the day.

- I leave secondary work for late in the afternoon.

- I goof off or have a relaxed day during the week.

- I work on Saturdays.

- I relax and renew on Sundays.

There is nothing sacred or amazing about these elements. They just work for me. Find your own elements and design your work week.

Two more points:

- I try to walk 10,000 steps a day for my physical health. It also creates a nice mental break for me. I usually head out to walk around 11:00 a.m. It takes about an hour and twenty minutes to get my steps in.

- I have learned to walk and read at the same time. A colleague turned me on to this decades ago. At first glance, I thought it was strange, even a little weird. But he gushed about how productive it was and how it made his reading less boring. My walking routine takes place in a local cemetery that has nicely paved roads that I know well. I also use a local campus running track to change things up a bit. The pathways are smooth, so I don't have to worry about tripping. I usually take one to three articles with me. I learned that I can't read anything complicated or philosophical because it's too hard to concentrate. Most of the articles are informative and centered around a set of topics I am interested in (e.g., leadership, teams, meetings, and transitions). It makes me feel productive and healthy at the same time. I learn something as well as keep in shape physically.

Appendix 2
My Favorite Five

These are my favorite five strategies that I use regularly to manage my procrastination habit. I have tried a whole lot of strategies, practices, and protocols, but this handful of ideas fall in my sweet spot.

> It's the job that's never started that takes longest to finish.
> —J. R. R. Tolkien

Rewards Are Effective, so I Use Them a Lot

I resisted the idea of rewards for a long time. My self-talk sounded like this: *I shouldn't need rewards to do what I need to do. I should be better/smarter/stronger than that.* It was stupid thinking. Use them they really work.

Thirty-Minute Work Periods Work for Me

Notice that I said they work *for me*. Some people might have to start with 10 or 20 minutes. Some might be able to do 45 or 60 minutes. Pay attention to what works for you. Don't fall into the trap of "I should" be able to work longer; that's self-sabotage.

It took many months of trial and error to figure out my sweet spot. I started by trying to do an hour at a time, and it just didn't work for me. My mind wandered all over the place. I fell into a lot of negative self-talk: *Why can't I concentrate for 60 minutes? What's wrong with me?* Find your true sweet spot, even if it's 15 minutes. If you can focus your efforts during your selected time frame, you will be very productive.

Visually Record Your Progress

Whether it's hours worked or rooms painted or receipts organized, mark your success and progress visually. I use bright yellow paper as my scorecard. It's something I can easily see and feel good about. Again, I resisted this notion initially. I had a lot of negative self-talk about it. But I tried it for a month and found it to be very helpful.

Temptation Bundling

When I heard about the temptation bundling technique, it was a revelation. For years, I had struggled with doing my income taxes. I learned by accident that if I watched a sports game while I did this onerous task, it *eventually* got done. Use temptation bundling whenever you can, *if* it works for you. It can neutralize the frustration, anxiety, and overwhelm we feel at the prospect of a noxious task. Do *not* get into the self-sabotage thinking that you "should" be able to punch through the task without any help or support. That is foolish thinking.

Eat the Small Frog First

Starting small was a counterintuitive notion for me. I was taught to eat the biggest frog first, and it never worked for me. It took a couple of decades—and a lot of pain and stress—to figure out otherwise, but once I made the switch, my procrastination habit diminished greatly.

The point here is to challenge common wisdom and do what works for you.

Appendix 3

Toolbox: Apps that Can Help Your Procrastination Habit

Procrastinators need all the help we can get. There are hundreds of apps that you can consider using. I will highlight about a dozen that I know to be quite effective.

- *Freedom*: This blocks distracting websites and apps on all platforms. It has a free trial; then you have to purchase a subscription.

- *Space*: In addition to blocking distracting apps, Space helps with your phone addiction so you can find some balance. Interestingly, the app identifies what type of phone user you are (with names like Boredom Battler, Social Sticky Mitt, and Rabbit Hole Wanderer). It's free and has in-app purchases.

- *Rescue Time*: This tracks how you actually spend your time, which can be very revealing. It's free for limited features and has a premium version.

- *Simple Habit*: This uses guided meditation to relive stress and anxiety. It's free for limited features and has a premium version.

- *Think Up*: This uses positive affirmations to give you a motivational boost when you need it. It's free for limited features and has a premium version.

- *Cold Turkey Blocker*: This blocks websites and applications on your computer and has additional features. It's completely free.

- *Forest*: This one is a little different. It helps you stay focused on the important things in life by planting a tree. When you focus and work on those things, your tree grows. If you don't—your tree dies!

- *Todoist*: This helps you organize, prioritize, and schedule all the tasks in your life. It's free for limited features and has a premium version.

- *Timebound*: This helps you keep track of all your deadlines by using a countdown clock for each one, with automated reminders. It's free.

- *Stop, Breathe & Think*: With this app, you get a daily mindfulness and meditation recommendation to help reduce your stress. It's free for limited features and has a premium version.

- *Habit Bull*: This tracks your habits and goals. It's free and has in-app purchases.

- *Block Site*: This blocks distracting websites on multiple platforms and helps control your browsing content.

- *White Noise Generator* (Android): This generates background sounds of your choice. It's free and has in-app purchases.

For the Truly Committed!

- *Beeminder*: This is a commitment device that establishes a consequence for failure. They charge you real money for not completing your agreed-upon task!

- *Stickk*: This is another accountability app with a coach and real money consequences involved.

- *Focus Mate*: This pairs you up with another person so you can get work done together.

Appendix 4
Words of Wisdom from the Stoics

I came across Stoicism several years ago though a conversation with a colleague who had just read the book *Essentialism* by Greg McKeown (2014). There are dozens of books about Stoicism, and it has become a popular way of life. What impresses me the most about the Stoics is that they created this branch of philosophy 2,000 years ago! I believe their wisdom and practicality have relevance in our complex and fast-paced world, where FOMO (fear of missing out) reigns supreme.

Below, I share some quotations from the Stoics for your consideration. I have several posted in my office as reminders when I get reactive and look for a diversion. Many of my colleagues and clients have some of these in their offices too, for motivation and support. I hope you find them helpful.

No one has anything finished because we have kept putting off into the future all our undertakings.

—Seneca

What is there, in this, that is unbearable and beyond endurance?

—Marcus Aurelius

Do external things distract you, then take time for yourself to learn
something worthwhile. Stop letting yourself be pulled
in all directions.

—Marcus Aurelius

Do everything as if it were the last thing you were doing in your
life and stop being aimless. Stop letting your emotions overrule what
your mind tells you.

—Marcus Aurelius

For those who might be interested in exploring the Stoics more
deeply, I recommend the following books:

- *The Beginner's Guide to Stoicism: Tools for Emotional Resilience
  and Positivity* (2019) by Matthew Van Natta

- *The Daily Stoic: 366 Meditations on Wisdom, Perseverance and
  the Art of Living* (2016) by Ryan Holiday and Stephen
  Hanselman

- *Meditations* by Marcus Aurelius

One Last Piece of Advice

Try just *one* thing and see what happens.

References

Allen, D. (2019). *Getting things done workbook*. Penguin Books.

Amabile, T. & Kramer, S. J. (2011). *The power of small wins*. Harvard Business Review.

Burka, J. & Yuan, L. M. (2008). *Procrastination: Why you do it, what to do about it* (2nd ed.). DaCapo Lifelong Books.

Chodron, P. (2013). *How to meditate: A practical guide to making friends with your mind*. Sounds True.

Clear, J. (2018). *Atomic habits: An easy and proven way to build good habits and break bad ones*. Avery.

Combs, J. (2011). *From procrastination to production: 7 steps to change your life now*. More Heart Than Talent Pub.

Duhigg, C. (2012). *The power of habit*. Random House.

Ferrari, J. (2010). *Still procrastinating: The no regrets guide to getting it done*. Wiley.

Fiore, N. (2007). *The now habit*. Tarcher Perigee.

Guise, S. (2013). *Mini habits: Smaller habits, bigger results*. Self-published.

Iyenga, S. (2011). *The art of choosing*. Twelve.

Karia, A. (2015). *Ready, set . . . procrastinate: 23 tools to stop procrastinating* (3rd ed.). Independent Publishing Platform.

Klein. G. (2007). *Conducting a premortem*. Harvard Business Review.

Pyshl, T. (2013). *Solving the procrastination puzzle*. Tarcher Press.

Salzgeber, N. (2017). Stop Procrastinating. Kindle Edition.

Schwartz, B. (2016). *The paradox of choice: Why less is more* (rev. ed.). Ecco Press.

Scott, S. J. (2017). *Habit stacking: 127 small changes to improve your health, wealth and happiness*.

Scott, S. J., (2018). *How to stop procrastinating*. Old Time Publishing.

Steel. P. (2012). *The procrastination equation*. Harper Perennial.

Tierney, J. (2011). Do you suffer from decision fatigue? *New York Times Magazine*.

Zahariades, D. (2020). *The procrastination cure: 7 steps to stop putting life off*. RWW Career.